A West Texas Soapbox

NUMBER TWO:
West Texas A&M University Series

A West Texas soapbox

JIM SANDERSON

Texas A&M University Press
College Station

First edition

The paper used in this book meets the minimum requirements
of the American National Standard for Permanence
of Paper for Printed Library Materials, Z39.48–1984.
Binding materials have been chosen for durability.
♾

Library of Congress Cataloging-in-Publication Data

Sanderson, Jim, 1953–
A West Texas soapbox / Jim Sanderson.
p. cm. — (Wext Texas A&M University series ; no. 2)
ISBN 0-89096-819-5
1. Texas, West—Civilization. 2. Frontier and pioneer life—
Texas, West. 3. Sanderson, Jim, 1953– . I. Title. II. Series.
F391.2.S26 1998
976.4'9—dc21 97-39446
CIP

Contents

Acknowledgments

There are people to thank. Ray Browne, the creator of the Popular Culture Association, encouraged me to keep writing these essays and published several. My buddy Terry Dalrymple, while editor of the *Concho River Review,* unwittingly contributed to this collection by publishing several essays. After a lot of rejections for this volume, I had given up on seeing these essays in book form, but Jerry Craven suggested that I send them to him. Jerry wore himself out trying to make me make myself clearer. I couldn't have had a better editor. Finally, I want to thank the sources for this collection: West Texans and West Texas, especially all drinking buddies, both male and female, both those who do and don't drink.

"Students and Looking Askance" appeared in abbreviated form in *Riversedge* (Edinburg, Tex.) (Spring 1992).

"Women and Texas" appeared in *The New Mexico Humanities Review* (Socorro, N.M.), no. 35 (1991).

"Art in the Desert" appeared in abbreviated form in *Journal of American Culture* (Bowling Green, Ohio), special edition, 14, no. 2 (Summer 1991) as "The American West as Image in Literature, Language, Painting, and Films," edited by Peter C. Rollins, Reed Harp, and Darin Cozzens.

"The Hispanic *Seduction* of the Southwest" appeared in abbreviated form in *The High Plains Literary Review* (Denver, Colo.), 5, no. 3 (Winter 1990/91).

"Old Corrals: Texas According to 80s Film and TV and According to Larry McMurtry" appeared in *Journal of American Culture* (Bowling Green, Ohio), 13, no. 2 (Summer 1990). Additionally, "Maintenance of the Texas Spirit in *The Yellow Rose*" appeared in *The Concho River Review* (San Angelo, Tex.) (Spring 1988), and "Texas Nostalgia in *Places in the Heart*" appeared in *The Concho River Review* (San Angelo, Tex.) (Spring 1987) (first volume).

"The Community College 'Philosophy' as Intellectual Pollutant" appeared in abbreviated form in *High Plains Literary Review* (Denver, Colo.), 4, no. 3 (Winter 1989/90).

"The Twentieth Century Frontier in Odessa, Texas: Bar Stools and Pulpits" is a revision printed upon invitation that appeared in *The Journal of American Culture* (Bowling Green, Ohio) (Winter 1987); a slightly different version appeared in *High Plains Literary Review* (Denver, Colo.) (Spring 1988).

Introduction

As a child, I could pick out a John Ford movie before I knew it was a John Ford movie—something about the way it looked and the characters dressed. In college, I studied western and Texas history and myth. Growing up in San Antonio, I realized that I was on the edge of the old Texas frontier line. When I moved to Odessa, well beyond that old frontier line, I found myself in the middle of the twentieth-century remnants of that history and myth.

I got interested in Ralph Waldo Emerson after I started graduate school. His "Nature" was a determining factor for American cultural consciousness. Emerson divided the world up into "Self" and what is not self, or "Nature." And at least in my understanding of Emerson, by paying attention to the senses, those qualities endemic to self, a person could go out into nature and lose self while simultaneously celebrating self. Walt Whitman expanded self in "Song of Myself" and became a part of Texas, as well as of all American history. Without Emerson and Whitman, we couldn't have romanticized the cowboy and the American West.

Later yet, while teaching sophomore literature, I happened across Norman Mailer's "The White Negro," in which the author praises psychopathy in two American existentialists: the Negro and the hipster. Mailer looks at the hipster as the white equivalent of the Negro, who "accepts the terms of death." The Negro, living outside of his own society that was and is dictated by white culture, lived constantly with death, or Uncle Tomism. So the Negro became the perfect existentialist, living for the orgiastic present. The hipster, and later the hippie, tried to reproduce this life. Both the hipster and the Negro listened to their psychopathic tendencies. Through listening to self-indulgent, psychopathic needs, the hipster, the Negro, and the rest of us have a chance for growth, a chance to work "backward" through our psychological (and/or sexual) handicaps and thus cure ourselves and see a reality unobstructed by perceptions other than our own. If he lives, a psychopath can save himself and perhaps the world. The cowboy is a psychopath.

With his admiration and endorsement of the psychopath in all of us, Mailer sounds somewhat like the American romantics of the nineteenth century. Emerson, like Mailer, had faith that the psychopath will prove more creative than destructive. Mailer's brand of existentialism may not be romanticism, but it is romantic. Though my philosopher friends may cringe and claim that I misinterpret existentialism, I see Mailer's existentialism as another form of American romanticism. The American renaissance was perhaps the discovery of Mailer's psychological quirk in American life. The neurotic, wimpy sailors on board the Pequod watch with fear and ineffectiveness as a greater individual, a psychopath named Ahab, leads them to knowledge and, unfortunately, to death. Hester Prynne goes out into the woods and ends up giving birth to her "witch baby" (Pearl) and defying her society. This repulsion yet fascination with the unrestrained individual, the id, the madman, proves to be fascinating to American minds and shows up as a recurring theme in American narratives. It becomes the basis of an American brand of tragedy: *Death of a Salesman, The Great Gatsby, Citizen Kane.* It is also apparent in the historic and mythical American West and in the historic and mythical Texas.

I found plenty of psychopaths and neurotics in Odessa—all psychological descendants from a frontier Texas. So almost as a game, I looked for the frontier myth, psychopathy and neurosis, and romanticism not in literature but in the life around me. Thus I wrote these essays as anecdotal examinations of life in West Texas. Here then, I rewrite these essays to give them some coherence and to divide them into comments about culture or education.

A West Texas Soapbox

The Twentieth-Century Frontier in Odessa, Texas

The cowboy, the miner, the mountain man—all extraordinary individuals in American myth—share a common need to escape society and its structures. Surly and independent, Davy Crockett and Daniel Boone left home and family for self-satisfying forages into the wilderness. Most mountain men and cowboys trapped beaver or herded cattle because they were psychologically unfit for much else. The American individual with all his attractive wildness is sociopathic in his flights from decent society and psychopathic in his self-indulgence. And to the frontiersmen, the land was not some manifestation of God. They were not sophisticated enough to see beyond the here and now. They simply accepted that life was tough. You had to sweat a lot, and you might die at any time. The farmers may have seen the spirit while looking at the land, but these men saw only the land.

The farmers followed the solitary wild men. While the cowboy is a romantic symbol of our spirit to us and to Europeans, the farmer who dragged his family with him is the chief sentimental symbol of our virtue. Even practical, Lockean Thomas Jefferson grows mushy when describing farmers: "Those who labour in the earth are the chosen people of God, if ever he had a chosen people, whose breasts he has made his peculiar deposit for substantial and genuine virtue." With the farmer, the feminine desires for home, church, and peaceful politics entered frontier communities.

In the famous scene from *My Darling Clementine* showing Henry Fonda and Cathy Downs dancing on the bare foundation of a church, movie director John Ford evokes what the church meant to wilderness society. In an isolated and wild area, the church brought not only spiritual comfort but political and social stability, recreation, community spirit, and entertainment. The church, like Jonathan Edwards's revivalist Puritan church, was an all-purpose idea and place.

To West Texas the farmers from East Texas and the rest of the American South brought the American South's Protestant God with them and thus expanded the borders of southern fundamentalism. They either chased the cowboys out or made uneasy alliances with them. They built churches and schools, eschewed the vulgarities of language, polished their Sunday school shoes and their boots.

Like most nineteenth-century romantics, the prairie Protestants who tried to make a living by farming in a semiarid area probably looked for God in nature. But the God that they saw in West Texas was not the harmonious, balanced God that Wordsworth saw in the pastoral English countryside or the southern God that they brought with them, but rather a rough, unbalanced God. Nature in West Texas was stark and distinct: jagged buttes rising out of flatness, seas of grass, heat, tornadoes, dryness. Their southern God took on the shape and the sparseness of their landscape. And, living in a land that is inhospitable and at times hostile to human presence, these West Texas farmers came to believe in a God of limitation, restriction, and punishment. In a religion that could not see tragedy and pathos and thus humanity, God became as prescriptive about life as the environment. He welcomed all followers but wanted them to lead a simple, limited, and restricted life. In the twentieth century, though the life has changed, the West Texas Protestant God has not.

Further, Baptist, Church of Christ (or Campbellite as some West Texans still say), Pentecostal, and Assembly of God Protestantism in twentieth-century West Texas does not have the same social or mythic effect as the incorporating, rank yet rich, European and Hispanic-influenced Catholicism. Without traditions or symbol, West Texas Protestant societies have neither the Catholic and thus Hispanic ability to see beauty in human misery, passion, and wildness nor the oriental ability to be amused by the absurdity of human desires. Fundamental Protestantism has trouble incorporating human pathos into its social and spiritual doctrine. Most fundamentalists just do not know what to do or think about the sexual and financial exploits of televangelists such as Jim Bakker or Jimmy Swaggert. Fundamentalists, descendants yet debunkers of strict Calvinism, do not know what to think or do about sin. Without a coherent philosophy, without the use of symbolism, with little sense of aesthetics, without a clear notion of sin, and with a harsh God giving prescriptions for salvation and living, these democratic denominations restrict and limit experience and behavior. Their leaders review high school textbooks and tell their members to stay out of bars, and some even banish music from church.

But in West Texas, early in the twentieth century, the frontier process reversed itself. With the oil booms in West Texas, the psychopathic, sociopathic, and earthy men who tended the rigs, who were the spiritual heirs to the nineteenth-century miner frontiersmen, met the farmers' daughters and eventually married them, the mutual attraction of opposites.

The feminine virtues of church and society initially won out. Still today in West Texas, church and the accompanying social mores try to determine the civilized thoughts of the populace and guard these thoughts from the subversive frontier, oil-field hearts. But the oil miner, while living in town and going to church, voted the county wet, still worked in the field, drank and whored with his buddies, and raised his sons to work in the oil fields, drink, and whore. Successive booms guaranteed that new generations of frontiersmen drifted to West Texas, and new social and psychological negotiations and conflicts began. Today, West Texas is a mixture of fundamentalism and frontierism. How a town or the individual mixes the two or chooses between them determines character.

By West Texas, I mean that vast expanse of barrenness just west of Walter P. Webb's ninety-eighth meridian, along some curving line bounded by the edge of the Hill Country on the east and by the Trans-Pecos area to the west. The Rio Grande from Big Bend to El Paso is too much like New Mexico or Arizona to be a part of flat, windswept, overgrazed West Texas. El Paso is too old, too much red rock desert to be West Texas, although eastern New Mexico and the towns that hug its border with Texas—Jal, Portales, Clovis, Hobbs—could be considered a part of oil-field West Texas. To me, after seven years of living in Odessa, the town and Odessans best exemplify the uneasy balance between fundamental strictures and frontier self-indulgence, between churches and bars.

In Odessa, West Texas, Andrews Highway gives a visitor the best view of the frontier remains in the town. For several miles Andrews Highway is lined with rusting oil equipment and small bars. The traditional oil man, like the miner, the cowboy, and the mountain man, would leave his good wife and good society to go off slumming in the wilderness to appease his psychopathic self-indulgence. His wife at home was a safety net, a place to fall in case his individuality carried him too far past the bounds of social acceptance or propriety or into self-absorption and loneliness. Today, instead of the wilderness or the boomtown, the West Texan frontiersman—or woman—has the bar and the reckless behavior that it offers.

These are not fern bars or country-western discos. They do not make much money, and they are not respectable. Whether these bars' customers are male or female, drinking in them is a masculine activity as much as churchgoing is feminine. Drinking is a delicious evil, done in real frontier-Baptist fashion: away from family and with disreputable friends. Meanwhile, *his* woman or her *man* is at home maintaining the ethics dictated by a fundamentalist, West Texas God.

So in Odessa, while the bars are full, Odessans see them as insidious. Odessans don't discuss bars in mixed company. Home and family are spiritually, socially, and politically endorsed. Marriage is a reliable civilizing influence. The Sunday newspaper's bridal page gets an exaggerated layout. Weddings, like Sunday services, serve as social gatherings. Bridal shops do good business and promote love, marriage, and "the most important day in a woman's life" through radio and TV ads. Local politicians all claim to be family men. Real-estate agents claim that communities are safe for a family and talk about starter homes. Odessans view single adults with suspicion. The single yuppie is not a native West Texan. Divorce also flourishes.

Odessans marry while in high school or two weeks after graduation. Young Odessans grow up hearing accolades for marriage that people in other parts of the country have come to distrust. Marriage further incorporates the soul-saving restrictions that the church finds necessary in West Texas. But the young folks only half believe what they hear, for young Odessans know the real truth: after high school the only real escape is to get married or get out of town. West Texans more so than other Americans are afraid of being alone. They live in an isolated community with bright lights, culture, and refinement three hundred miles away in Dallas, Austin, or San Antonio. So unless young Odessans plan to pack off to college and perhaps desert their heritage, their only option is to marry. The isolation and harshness that caused their great grandparents to see a tough Protestant God cause the young West Texans to plan for marriage.

After marriage begins to weigh heavily on the couple, the obvious solution to marital problems is to have children. Malls in Odessa are crowded with young women with babies. And once the aging Odessans find themselves confined into families, the old self-indulgent urge for wildness pulls many toward the bars. The bars' patrons and atmosphere—the dark, frontier side of West Texas's heritage, the forbidden fruit of twentieth-century Protestantism—seduce many couples.

Odessans will cling to a marriage because society, church, and advertising endorse it as the only lifestyle leading to happiness. Married Odessans find their blissful dreams disturbed by a contented single person. If someone can find happiness within this isolation and austerity without a partner, then perhaps a wife could find happiness without a man, a husband without a woman; so married Odessans are quick to console their obviously miserable single friends.

Still, Odessans are notorious for affairs and divorces, which become either exhilarating or tortured attempts to capture a frontier self that was lost to the restrictions of marriage. Indulging in affairs and divorce is a delicious evil that mixes well with liquor. And sometimes, especially for women, the local colleges, with older-than-average student populations, offer the chance for some vicarious wildness through education.

Many Odessans identify fundamentalism with free enterprise. Owning a business is a socially sanctioned extension of individuality and frontiersmanship. An Odessan is far better off with his own firm than with a divorce or with a reserved spot at a bar. In a city dominated by Dairy Queens, Long John Silver's and McDonald's fast-food establishments, and other Mcbusinesses, many people often start their own enterprises. The overborrowing that helped cripple the West Texas oil industry resulted from a Texas-style mixture of church with frontier mentality and greed.

No discussion of business and the oil boom and West Texas would be complete without at least a cursory glance at Odessa's neighbor fifteen miles to the east: Midland. Another example of West Texas development and of American corporatism, though unlike working-class Odessa, Midland is the home of the white-collar accountants and managers in the oil industry. Midland bills itself as the "Tall City" because it has a business district with four or five high-rises. To the north of these buildings is the rest of Midland, and to the east and south is mostly empty land. Rather than expanding out into vacant lots, Midland expanded up, like Dallas or New York, and thereby created parking garages and traffic jams. The West

Texas God looks down and smiles upon corporatism, which Midlanders confuse with free enterprise, and corporatism can be comforting. Claiming to be a Texan, but an obvious Yankee who did his time in Midland, former president George Bush is a good example of a Midlander. Midlanders say that you raise kids in Midland and raise hell in Odessa. Bush probably never drove over to Odessa.

But God needs more than just business to guard Odessa. A group called Odessans For Decency shows the extreme of Odessans' equation of Americanism, religion, and business. Members of Odessans For Decency, who sometimes find their parent group (Americans For Decency) too liberal, seek to protect local Christian, governmental, and capitalistic values from media liberalism, pornography sold in convenience stores, and encroaching socialism. During my stay in Odessa, the leader of this group was a small-business man, an insurance salesman. In order to preserve Christian values and free enterprise, members of Odessans For Decency liked to picket businesses: mostly medical clinics performing abortions and convenience stores.

Ironically, a true, unreconstructed frontier oil man sneers at those who own businesses in town. Tending shop won't make a man sweat; it isn't work. And if a man wants to escape work, he is better off as a paper-shuffling bureaucrat, librarian, teacher, or some other feminine and church-endorsed worker. The bar patrons first looked at my "perfesser" friends who preceded me into the bars as strange, unmanly creatures. But several of my professor friends assured me that when the local bar patrons "realized" that professing was a way to fake respectability, to get off work and start drinking by midafternoon, and to ogle all sorts of young bodies, they preached harder to their kids to stay in school and study hard.

Because of the mix of fundamentalism and frontierism, Odessans are well armed. Even good women carry pistols now because of an organization called Women Armed For Self Protection. Kindly, elderly ladies in this group tell reporters that they pack a piece and know how to use it. Jeffersonian agrarianism gradually became corrupted into the mythic nineteenth-century farmer, who owned a plow, a wagon, and a rifle and nightly read his Bible. The cowboy had a pistol, which, incidentally, if carried at all, was used to shoot only rattlesnakes and oftentimes disintegrated in his holster. But the modern Odessa frontiersman still thinks of his pistol as a tool. It is his means of defending his home and family against "them," some hazy enemy. Perhaps, with his pistol packed away in a closet or under the seat of his car (and now, with Texas's recently passed concealed gun law, he can pack his piece in his pocket), he defends his woman and his fundamentalism from wild, self-indulgent frontierism. Thus to be consistent, he would have to shoot himself. Fortunately, suicide is not a problem in Odessa; few Odessans shoot themselves because of the guilt they feel for transgressions in bedrooms and bars. Usually they shoot other Odessans.

Unreconciled fundamentalism and frontierism in an individual oftentimes result in violence, and Odessa is, for a fact, a violent place. During the boom, when I first arrived in Odessa, it had just beaten Miami as the nation's murder capital, as having the most murders per capita. I am surprised that Odessa is not *more* violent.

The shootings in Odessa are not the outcome of passionate family squabbles but rather the result of unbalanced men trying to reconcile their wildness with their fundamentalist morality. The unreconciled or unrealized tension between individuality and community, feminine and masculine impulses, wildness and acceptability—all caused by the frontier remnants represented best by church and bar—cause a lot of Odessans to drink, to divorce, to marry, to toil excessively at doomed businesses, and to shoot each other.

Fancying myself a Tocqueville in boots, I'd like to state some prejudices clearly. The West Texan must come to terms with the civilizing and self-indulgent aspects in himself and his environment to approach any sense of peace or awareness. With a busted oil boom and a state in turmoil about its own identity, Texans perhaps are drifting closer toward a communal identity rather than self-identity. We can no longer see ourselves as individuals or act out an unrestrained individualism. Neither can we let the restrictions of a worn-out social and religious view dominate our social standards or sense of community. We need a kinder, gentler social and religious view.

But I still want to be a cowboy.

Recently, a hometown native, while still a hot political prospect, said that Texans will inevitably have to move toward communal identity rather than an unhindered individualism or frontier identity. Shortly after this proclamation, this politician was caught in an affair with his campaign manager. Meanwhile, his wife was praying and going to faith healers, seeking a cure for the defective heart of her newborn son. I don't mean to make fun of him, I admire him, but a wiser, more progressive, more literate, more Hispanic-Catholic, South Texas version of the conflict that I describe here caught him. He knows that a new communal view has to emerge—it means progress—but he is driven by its antithesis.

Perhaps this drift will take some of the edges off our flinty West Texas frontiersmanship. But I don't want to see the bar stool surrender to the pulpit or its modern, more progressive forces. More sophisticated Texans would call these people propped up on bar stools "rednecks." Such "rednecks" sometimes possess the creativity equivalent to the fledgling artists that critics, publishers, and gallery owners praise in Houston, Dallas, and Austin. These West Texans are just preartistic, if not preverbal. Their ironic and absurdist view of life and abundant energy are a developmental stage away from the fledgling artists.

As a teacher, I prefer the frontiersman in my students over the Protestant fundamentalist. The good Christians are good students but don't learn much. They make grades. God, country, and English teachers are all symbols of authority, so they do or think what these symbols tell them to do. Their goal is to complete and compete; it is not to learn. They strive to fit in but do not question; thus despite their ability, their goals are contrary to the demands of self-awareness. In a world literature class, the good Baptist students applauded my meager introduction to the Reformation. Refusing to see the Reformation as a political or cultural event, they viewed it as the emergence of the good guys who had a slight inkling of the right religion.

These students who insist on seeing only black and white, good and evil eventually get to be civic-minded citizens who equate art and religion. The Odessa Chamber of Commerce likes to brag about Odessa's replica of the Globe Theater (of course the Chamber also brags about the statue of the giant jackrabbit). The Globe is dedicated to only good, "family" fare: a Shakespeare festival, gospel singing contests, a commissioned play about the glory of Odessa, and Christian melodramas.

Having left Odessa, I went back and appeared at the replica of the Anne Hathaway cottage adjacent to the Globe. I had returned to Odessa for a fiction reading, but I *heard* that Odessa College administrators, most good Christian community members who had recently lost the college's operating budget through investments in derivatives, had deemed me too controversial to appear on campus. Perhaps the administrators subtly let it be known that I was not welcomed back because of articles such as this one.

Perhaps not; perhaps what I heard was just an unfounded rumor; perhaps they didn't even remember me. I don't remember them ever reading anything that I wrote. At any rate, some friends scheduled my appearance at the shrine to Shakespeare and religion. I preached to the choir—my friends and former students—and thus didn't infect anyone, and drank some beer afterward. Meanwhile the president was in the process of resigning and becoming a lay minister, and the vice president of finance who came up with the idea of investing in derivatives had been found out and fired by other corporations and was completing truck-driving school.

Unlike good Christian students and civic-minded administrators, the troubled, rebellious, contemptuous oil folk, who are distrustful of drama and other art forms, have the spirit if not always the ability to grow intellectually. People who choose Odessa bar stools over seats at the Globe or the local church know about sin and human suffering. An old oil field hand will show you his missing fingers or, like London Johnson, lift up his shirt to show you his mean looking surgical scars and say, "That's where the metal bit me."

As is usually the case, bar patrons can explain themselves far better than I can. "When I was young, my eyes was blue, and my peter was red," Pete Proctor and Tyree, former regular drinkers at Marie's Drive In, always used to say. "I was a handsome man. But now my eyes are red, and my peter is blue." Tyree liked to say that they got "thick on's" once in a while. Poor old Pete was crippled up, and T. Tyree had no teeth and a sick wife. "T." is just what everybody called him, since no one liked the name Thomas.

Evelyn, the sixty-year-old waitress at Marie's, who had broken both her wrists and one ankle in car wrecks, told T. Tyree and me about the old prostitute who came into Marie's. The prostitute told Evelyn that she had "done" so many old men that she could play pool with a rope. T. Tyree said you got more agile when you got old: "Making love," T. said, his lips folding into his mouth, "was like putting an oyster in a parking meter." T. waited, looked seriously at us, his mouth open, lips slightly apart; then his lips again curled over his gums, and he cackled.

T. Tyree, like most West Texas barroom cowboys, was originally from someplace else. Tyree grew up in a large aristocratic family in Virginia. He joined the service during World War II and was one of the first pilots to take off from and land bombers on an aircraft carrier. Later he was stationed at Rattlesnake Air Base in Peyote, Texas (you can still see the dilapidated hangar, which was at the time the largest in the country, sticking out from the mesquite that has grown over the deserted air base). T. also met the woman he would lovingly refer to as "Mama" during his stay in the oil fields. So after the war, rather than return to his green Virginia landscape, he stayed in flat, scraggly Odessa and got a job in the oil fields and married Mama. Like many easterners, he must have been fascinated and scared of the open sky. After so many years, like a westerner, a plainsman, T. would get claustrophobic when surrounded by green trees, and a cloudy sky.

There are legends about T. Tyree. During the boom shortly during and after World War II, he, a good-looking young man with all his teeth, was said to have "busted up more homes than World War I." One new guy on T.'s oil rig crew had a brand-new cowboy hat with a feather in the side. Something about the dandyism of a feather pissed T. off, so as the new guy took off his hard hat and put on his feathered hat, T. lit the feather with his Zippo.

Years later in Marie's, retired, hair slicked back under a silver-belly Stetson with a few dark stains at the base of the crown, T. would sip Budweisers from a small bar glass. He would cackle at our jokes and accuse us of lying. We had to listen closely because, with no teeth, he couldn't fully form his words. After he told his sexual, scatological, navy, and oil-field jokes, he'd go home precisely at six, after exactly three Budweisers, to fix dinner for Mama—"elsewise she'll hit me with the frying pan for chasing split-tails." T. would have been welcomed in the Pentecostal church across from Marie's Drive In if he didn't go to Marie's.

When the three-story Pentecostal church opened up across from Marie's, the good Christian congregation tried to evoke a city ordinance stating that a bar couldn't open within five hundred yards of a church. But Marie's had been established first and had an older tradition in Odessa than the Pentecostal church. Also, Marie regularly paid her taxes.

Marie and her younger husband, Bill, sat off at the corner of the bar just where it curved toward the back room. Sipping a cheap beer, staring at patrons, eyes seeming to bulge behind thick glasses, Marie at first scared the hell out of you. But after a year or two of your steady business, she'd welcome you into her bar.

Old-time drinkers like to tell about the time that Cliff, a long, skinny patron who looked like a Tennessee volunteer in the old Civil War photos, took Maxine, a regular drinker and friend of Evelyn's, home because she got drunk waiting for her boyfriend to show up. Once Cliff got her home, Maxine got confused about whom she was with, and Cliff got lucky. A day later, when Maxine found out what she had done, she went back to Marie's and offered anybody who would listen two hundred dollars to shoot Cliff. Nobody wanted to shoot Cliff, and Maxine later forgave him.

Mamma Rudd had the longest running bar in Odessa, Rudd's #2; the bar opened in 1941. There is no #1; #2 means that Mamma Rudd changed her operation from a grill to a bar. When I last saw her, Mamma Rudd was eighty-six and had yellow-tinted eyes. She would sit on a bar stool in her bar drinking Schlitz and nibbling from a block of cheese. She refused to shop at a grocery store that did not sell beer, and she bought her beer, not from her bar, but from the grocery store with the best price on Schlitz.

Mamma Rudd used to allow the whores into Rudd's back when it was a grill, and they conducted some of their business there. "Whores," Mamma Rudd liked to say, "have no souls." They just look like people but aren't really human beings. She told me about her husbands. Back in Oklahoma one ran off and left her with two kids, forcing her to move to Odessa. Another husband died. Another divorced her. She said that she never loved any of them, but she married because in those times a husband was a business necessity. She needed a man to help her get the bank loans or to add on to the bar. She told her son Charlie Bedford, who ran the bar for her, that he had better stop chasing married women because both they and their husbands were mean and worthless. "I'll tell you about goddamn love. The best thing a man ever did for me was die," she once said to me. I've never met anyone who was as hard and as tough as Mamma Rudd. I often wondered about the agonized frontier existence she had had and thus the price she had paid for her toughness.

On Christmas Eve in 1988 the husband of Charlie Bedford's girlfriend found out about them, came into Rudd's, said "Merry Christmas," stretched his arm over a customer's shoulder, and emptied the chamber of his pistol into Charlie. Mamma Rudd wasn't in the bar to see the killing, but later, with Charlie Bedford gone, she had to be sent to an "old folks home." T. Tyree died before I left. Pete Proctor stopped going into Marie's because his legs stopped working. The doctor told Evelyn that she might as well keep smoking and drinking until the end because her cancer was so far advanced. I saw Evelyn on a return visit to Odessa, and she matter-of-factly told me about her cancer. I was glad that I was not around to see her dwindle. Marie died, but her place is still making money, and Bill now has several girlfriends.

The laconic, self-effacing sentiment and humor of Pete and T., their clever inversions of language and logic, and their sexist, sexual, and scatological yarns are more entertaining than most of the Christian fare playing down at the Globe and far more creative than the *A* essays of churchy students. From selfishness, sociopathy, and psychopathy comes more potential for creativity and thought than from respect for social, cultural, and moral authority.

In the real world of politics and power, Texas's character is shaped in several humid cities: Dallas, San Antonio, Houston, and Austin. Maybe, as Larry McMurtry claimed in his 1981 *Texas Observer* article "Ever a Bridegroom: Reflection on the Failure of Texas Literature," the Texas writer should examine dynamic, complex urban Texas. But then, McMurtry went back to a mythic rural Texas in arguably his best and certainly most popular novel, *Lonesome Dove.* The Texans in the real world of humid cities east of I-35 are busy trying to create copies of other major American cities, but the dry urban frontiers out beyond Walter P. Webb's ninety-eighth meridian, because of their past isolation and relatively late development, still cling to the remains of the frontier. Unlike the urban, sometimes international, immigrants to San Antonio, Austin, Dallas, and Houston, the rural, native immigrants to Lubbock, Amarillo, Midland, Odessa, and Big Spring are less ready to surrender a frontier strain in their paradoxical natures.

West Texas and these West Texas cities may be the life support system for what the frontier has evolved into. And despite the openness, the humor, and the unintentional honesty in this patient, perhaps the life support system needs to be turned off. For like most other beliefs or attitudes in America, West Texas's residual frontier spirit creates destructive paradoxes in American psyches.

As evidenced by the passing of Marie, Mamma Rudd, and T. Tyree, maybe the patient is already gone. The present generation seems to have lost an emotional attachment to the frontier or the myth that arose out of it. The diluted myth no longer carries the kind of cultural and nearly religious response necessary to make a force in people's lives. Instead, in West Texas the myth has evolved into a mentality or an ideology. It is a strict manner of thinking and reacting to the world. It no longer has the pain, the introspection, and the cultural binding of a myth. In Marie and T. the residual frontier myth produced an attitude, a humor, and certain reticent tolerance of *some* people and ideas. To younger West Texans (maybe to all Texans) now a long way from a frontier, the residue of myth produces a knee-jerk response to life's struggles, choices, and dilemmas.

But it is the paradox and mentality that make West Texas a fitting study for the historian and maybe a fitting home for the writer. Writers should find West Texas rich in material. The mixture of these two frontier strains—religion and reckless frontiersmanship—creates a rich assortment of conflicts that seem to be reflected even in the landscape and the weather. Writers, always observers rather than participants when they do their job, have in West Texas examples of what they most use: passion and pathos.

If we are to accept the logic of Henry Nash Smith, Leo Marx, and Frederick Jackson Turner, we should accept the psychological conditioning of our diluted and fading myths and their effect on our history. If the frontier is indeed the cause of much of our nature, then certainly those places with a frontier past reflect our national nature. West Texas, then, particularly Odessa, with its skewered frontier process and resulting mixture of religion and frontiersmanship, may be ripe ground for the writer, sociologist, psychologist, historian, or political scientist to gather data for interpreting what it means to be an American in the twentieth century and maybe the twenty-first century.

Art in the Desert

In West Texas, *bullshit* is not really a bad or vulgar word. It has a richness to it that few proper words could match. A good West Texan knows that "bullshit" or the act of "bullshitting" or a "bullshitter" has some charm or interest. It is the basis of poetry. It is fun. It should not be confused with "horseshit" (pronounced "hars-hit"), a mean lie devoid of charm or interest. Neither is it "dogshit," a completely worthless product. "Chickenshit" applies to a flaw in people or institutions. Most churchgoers, civic leaders, college administrators, and strict intellectuals don't like bullshit.

Many West Texans, like many Texans and Americans, don't like pure bullshit. They don't see any complexities in their myths whether those myths are Texan or American. These West Texans want faith and profundity, not the fun of bullshitting. Again, myth becomes a mentality. So Odessans adhere strongly to community college "philosophy," capitalism, Jesus, or Texas pride. Or they just as strongly oppose such concepts. With more introspection would come deeper and more complex feeling and faith. A firmer appreciation of art would help since art examines the myth and sometimes remythifies the myth. It provides complexity. Unfortunately, most people in the desert, in Odessa, a town that had as its motto "Odessa is Crude," don't see any use in art. In Odessa, I was constantly asked what you can use literature for. Ironically, this frontier crudity is the basis for a lot of endemic Texas art.

In 1888 Henry James assessed Americans' attitudes about art in "The Art of Fiction":

> *"Art," in our Protestant communities, where so many things have got so strangely twisted about, is supposed in certain circles to have some vaguely injurious effect upon those who make it an important consideration, who let it weigh in the bal-*

ance. It is assumed to be opposed in some mysterious manner to morality, to amusement, to instruction. When it is embodied in the work of the painter (the sculptor is another affair!) you know what it is: it stands there before you, in the honesty of pink and green and a gilt frame: you can see the worst of it at a glance, and you can be on your guard. But when it is introduced into literature it becomes more insidious — there is danger of its hurting you before you know it.

Henry James had never been to West Texas; in 1888 there would have been few people and less art for him even to judge, but with his statement he shows a glimpse of the future. Twentieth-century American fundamental Protestant art criticism reached West Texas and further confused West Texans about art.

What James couldn't see, though, was that in the twentieth century most Americans (especially fundamentalists in religion, politics, or education), would stop reading. To those few Americans who do buy books, sometimes even me, *nonfiction* is the source of controversial and important opinions. But poetry and fiction just cloud issues, they lie. For, as James continues, "Literature should either be instructive or amusing, and there is in many minds an impression that these artistic preoccupations, the search for form, contribute to neither end, interfere indeed with both. They are too frivolous to be edifying and too serious to be diverting; and they are moreover priggish and paradoxical and superfluous."

On the other hand, visual art is out where any newborn innocent of whatever age might see it. Odessans assume that vision is some sort of public domain, like the airwaves, and thus that vision must not be impaired with smut masquerading as art. Art is bluebonnet paintings, Easter pageants, and John Wayne movies. So, surprisingly to me, Odessans are very concerned about "art pictures."

In the summer of 1984 Odessans For Decency banded together with other Decency organizations across the South and Southwest to picket Seven Elevens for allowing *Playboy* and *Penthouse* in their stores. Such magazines are particularly odious to Decency people because the pictures on the covers and in the centerfolds entice nonreaders to look inside and see the insidious words that accompany the pictures. Further, these magazines were displayed so that any person, even a child, walking innocently into a convenience store for a Slurpy and a pack of M&M's might come eyeball to breast with Miss September. These Odessans fear that pornography, which sometimes masquerades as art, has such power that if a person, especially a youngster, sees it, he will try it.

I had just gotten back from several weeks in Taos, New Mexico, where no one worried about the literature and pictures in convenience stores, and noticed Odessan mothers wheeling their children in front of the Seven Eleven closest to me. The Decency mothers had signs plastered to their strollers and to their kids: "I don't want to read porn"; "Keep porn away from me"; "Don't pollute my child." I bought a carton of milk, a *Playboy,* and two copies of the same issue of *Penthouse.* Then I walked in front of the mothers with my milk under my arm and stared at the centerfolds. They turned up their noses like they had smelled a turd (as my Odessan drinking buddies would say).

At this time, I learned that the Odessans For Decency had something to say about most local issues, even if they were ignorant of the issues. Like terrorists and soda water advertisers, they craved media attention. I also learned that their leader was an insurance salesman, George Franklin.

I met George a little over a year after the protests against nasty magazines in Seven Elevens. In October of 1985, my friend, Odessa College artist Barry Phillips, displayed the works of artist Larry Travis of U.T. Arlington. Previously, Barry had to pull down the collages of Amarillo artist Denny Fraze because he took images of our Lord in vain. He juxtaposed traditional religious paintings with other images. Now Barry had displayed sex. In pink and green expressionism, right there before the innocent, just a bit fuzzy, was a woman with her fingers dangerously near a nasty part of her body. *Thinking Of You Ziggi* was the title. Students complained, faculty members (to my surprise) complained, and O.C. staff complained. But not until the Decency people showed up with a TV reporter did O.C. administrators put the painting in question into a closet. The TV stations and the newspaper carried the story. The vice president of academic affairs claimed that the painting was not taken down but rather just relocated—in a closet.

At the time, I was writing movie reviews for the *Odessa American,* so with the encouragement of the editor, I tried to explain art to Odessans within the limitations of my column and knowledge and their attention spans. Thus a journalism war started. The opinion page carried letters that sided with me and others that condemned me. Most, like the letter from the secretary of Odessans For Decency, asked what he thought were rhetorical questions (I couldn't figure out what his questions were getting at) and quoted liberally from the Bible to disprove my citation of William Faulkner. (Faulkner died in 1962, the letter pointed out, but Christ was still living. So who are we to believe?) To groups like the Decency people, rhetorical questions and Bible quotes defeat any argument. I also got a slew of letters at Odessa College, some shoved under my office door. Most of these writers were sure that I was a communist, liberal, atheist, or, worst of all, a humanist. Most of the writers were sure that I was going to hell but pleaded with me not to damage the minds of the young people whom I taught and thus take them with me. Most, though, promised to pray for me.

George didn't write anything; I'm not sure that he could write. My editor told me that George had called him and wanted him to print a rebuttal to me in my next column. My editor told George that his giving George my column was like letting him into my living room to piss on my sofa. So George came to my office to talk to me. He thought that we were probably both just good fellas and could see eye to eye. What is more, he had brought his porn movie collection with him. He wanted the government instructor down the hall to watch the porn movies with him to see if they were indeed *legally* pornographic, and since I was a movie critic, he wanted me to watch the movies with him to see if they were indeed *artistically* pornographic. I had an image of a constitutional expert, the local movie reviewer, and a staunch Christian sitting in the dark and wringing their sweaty palms together while they watched pictures that were far "dirtier" than the one that caused the debate. I was tempted to watch the movies with George. But both the government instructor and I refused George's offer. I offered George a list of my favorite porn titles. He then came into my office to see if we couldn't discuss the problem and clear up our differences.

George asked if I didn't think that a "picture" of a woman with a finger in her rectum was pornographic. I told George that I didn't see the "picture" because his people had had it removed. "George," I added, "I heard the finger was nearer her vagina. And before you go around pulling pictures down, you better get your orifices straight."

George looked at me blankly, "What difference does it make what she had her finger in?"

I then told George that, from what I understood, the painting was satiric. It was saying to the viewer that, whenever we look at a woman, because of our society, we see only sex. Thus we are all pornographers.

George shook his head and then said, "What is this satire thing you people keep talking about? Can you explain it to me?" I preferred not to explain satire to George but referred him to our second-semester freshman English textbook. Later George asked me the question that he was really concerned about. George looked me squarely in the eye and lowered his voice to ask, "Jim, are you a Christian?"

"I wish that I could stop being a Christian," I said intently, "but I can no more stop being a Christian than you can stop being a Greek Humanist, George." I then went on to say that Western civilization was the story of the integration of Judeo/Christian faith with Greek ideas and later with the ideas arising out of the Enlightenment. I added that we just cannot escape our culture. George's eyes wrinkled together as he tried to retrace what I said in order to figure out the point at which he got lost. His mouth tried to shape some words in the form of another question, but he didn't know what to ask. He thanked me and left.

I could figure out why George Franklin's group got irritated at Larry Travis's paintings, but I was dumbfounded as to why so many Odessans were upset at Barry Phillips's praise of Andy Warhol. When Warhol died, Barry wrote a short commemorative letter to the editor of the *Odessa American* about Warhol's importance in the art world. Immediately Odessans sent in articles vehemently objecting to Warhol and to Barry. Some took a smug, superior attitude and argued that Barry and other foggy-headed intellectuals were taken in by Warhol. This was proof again that common folk know a whole lot more about art than intellectuals, academicians, or even artists.

I think that Warhol scared the bluebonnet and cowboy painters and those blue-haired ladies still trying to mix flesh tones. These are not necessarily the Decency people. Rather than a rigid morality, these people have a rigid aesthetic. They may not know much about art, but they know what they like. And what they like, as hazy as it is, gives them a mind-numbing comfort rather than a sense of beauty. Warhol, whether he is or will be recognized as a great artist, is a threat because he challenges this contentment.

Many Texans see art only as a means to confirm what they deem far more important than art. To these Texans, art leads to nobility and goodness and validates old prejudices about self. Though they don't know what to do with artists, these Texans put those who deal with the fine arts or the liberal arts in the same sanitized position as the preacher or the self-help psychology book author (thus devout Christians and devout bluebonnet painters blaspheme artists by putting them in the company of do-gooders and preachers). Art should thus follow prejudices and status quo and not ask questions. Art too is somehow personal and subjective, so it really has no rules. What I like is as good as what is good. What I like or what I already believe is good, and anything that doesn't conform to what I like is bad. So with no rules, art needs social good or community values to guide it and look after it for its own sake. Further, art and religion have their proper places. As Mrs. May says in Flannery O'Connor's "Greenleaf," "Jesus should be kept inside the church building like other words inside the bedroom." Print, because no one reads, can keep itself locked up; the visual arts cannot.

Thus in Odessa, sex, religion, and art are sanitized and abstracted. If anyone dares render the abstraction concrete, then he produces pornography or blasphemy. The 1988 movie release of *The Last Temptation of Christ* tested Odessans' resolves and became the next visual controversy. Conditioned to an abstract Jesus, local folks rejected this concrete Jesus. The good Christians of Odessa wanted a wimpy, pink-eyed, perfect Jesus with no human or divine blood in him, like Max Von Sydow in George Stevens's *The Greatest Story Ever Told* (John Wayne was even in this one, flubbing his lines as a centurion). But in Martin Scorsese's *The Last Temptation of Christ,* Willem Dafoe, as a wild-eyed Jesus, hangs naked on the cross, his genitalia magnified, and dreams about sex with Barbara Hershey. Like the townfolk of Hadleyburg in Mark Twain's story, the good Odessans wanted salvation without temptation, without sensual alternatives. In Odessa the minister of *education* at the First Baptist Church of Odessa commented on the movie's artistic merits to the newspaper, and the First Baptist's hefty secretary appeared on the front page of the newspaper with a scowl on her face and a petition to keep the movie out of Odessa. So well did the minister of education's cinematic and aesthetic sensibilities serve him, he was able to discover that the film had no "artistic merit" without even seeing the film. Unlike George Franklin, he was unwilling to cast his eyes upon his enemies. The minister knew that Odessans have all the real art that they need on CBN, and he was able to discern, again without seeing the film, that it was "not based on fact." No one objected to Nikos Kazantzakis's novel resting on a shelf in the Ector County library.

Even nonfundamentalists were scared by this movie, which rendered the sacred as sensual to make the myths we live by more powerful. Mario Cuomo, hardly a fundamentalist Texan, refused to see the movie. Closer to home, the Dallas city council voted to denounce the film. The film did play for the leftover hippies and the humanists in Austin. Luckily, since nobody in Odessa was Moslem, or could admit to being a Moslem, no one objected to fleshing out Mohammed in *The Satanic Verses.* But again, this was only a fictional book, and thus not real. Some people who tried to keep *The Last Temptation of Christ* out of Odessa defended Salmon Rushdie's freedom of speech. Ultimately, United Artists' Dallas distributors decided what was best for Odessa and kept the film out of town.

Other Odessans were indifferent to the art debates. They reflected the view of the legislator who said in front of the 1987 Texas legislature, "The Arts are only a welfare project for the rich." Most of my students, reflecting national assumptions, equated art with entertainment. And entertainment, to these people, is a bromide. The most popular art form, the place where most people get their dose of art, is film. *The Last Temptation of Christ* would probably have offended these moviegoers because it aims to be more than an escape and thus probably grows boring.

The Movie Channel stops people coming out of films and asks them what they think of movies. The usual response is that the movies help them escape, as though in a movie theater these viewers can somehow fall off the world or grow brain dead and plug into a life support system. To most moviegoers for whom art equals entertainment and entertainment equals escape, the way to measure escape is the amount of laughter. Aristotle's "delight" takes place in the present age, not through the excitement of pity and fear, but only through comedy, usually slapstick. Thus the more laughs and the louder the laughs then the better the picture and the wiser the movie consumer. The mass of moviegoers laugh at critics, at tension, and at tragedy. They daren't not laugh, dare not admit that they weren't entertained because they would then have to admit that the movie was lousy and that they were lousy consumers.

One of the first movies that I saw in Odessa was Sydney Lumet and David Mamet's *The Verdict.* A tense courtroom drama with few laughs, the movie's most dramatic moment occurs when the drunken lawyer hero, Paul

Newman, discovers that his new lover and assistant, Charlotte Rampling, has been helping his opposition. Not able to help himself, Paul Newman doesn't just slap Charlotte Rampling but coldcocks her. The Odessa audience started cheering and laughing. I got nervous.

As a newspaper critic, I learned that many people read my column so that they knew what not to go see. They got used to my tastes and avoided anything that I recommended and went to anything that I lambasted. For this reason, the theater managers liked me. I helped box office draw because I didn't like much.

Some people actually resented the fact that I sat in the dark and took notes. One lady, during a feature that I was watching, poked her husband in the ribs and pointed at me. I heard him whisper to her to leave me alone. As the end credits started to roll, she could resist no longer. She asked me what on earth I was doing. I told her that I was taking notes. She nodded her head as though she understood, scooted closer to her husband, and urged him to leave before this pervert who took notes in the dark did something really strange.

On another occasion some teenage thugs, the kind who usually gather in gangs outside of mall theaters, saw me taking notes in the dark. They began making catcalls to me and taunting me. They seemed to dare me to pay more attention to the movie than to them. I got up and moved farther away. They just grew louder. At the end of the movie, as people filed out of the theater, they waited at the entrance and yelled, "Hey movie critic, was it good? Was it good? Thumbs Up?" I ducked out the side door to avoid a fight.

With such people going to the movies and such amoral people investing in them, I really got disenchanted with American movies. Pragmatic and crass moviemakers know that they can manipulate and fool most people with quick and easy laughs instead of substance or craft, so they make quick, easy movies. They know that the moviegoers are afraid to admit that they have seen a lousy movie.

But people's assumptions about film cause deeper problems for America than lousy movies. Odessans, like most Americans, assume that what we see is more objective and more real than what we read, so why read? A picture, we assume, especially if it is a moving one presented by Dan Rather, is more revealing than print. Film became a narrative medium before it was even considered as a documentary medium because it is highly emotional. Every time a camera catches an image—because of lighting, composition, editing, and camera angle—it makes an emotional statement. Because the viewer does not have to go through a layer of words, as does the reader, the image is far more direct and thus more dramatic and emotional than print. Yet we get most of our news from TV because we figure that those pictures that accompany Dan Rather's voice are the "objective" truth.

So whether moviegoers, art patrons, occasional readers, or just interested observers, many Odessans who concern themselves with art, who let it weigh in the balance, make the same mistake: they confuse form with content. They equate the form that they have been conditioned to see or read—whether realistic art, chronological narrative, or invisible American film editing—with truth. They impose these forms upon their world to shape that world into a comfortable image. Though the rhetorical or artistic act assumes a graspable truth, the form is merely the means of conveying that truth; it is not the objective truth itself. All of these objections to films or paintings have more or less been objections to form—Willem Dafoe's nakedness, expressionistic nudes, soup cans instead of bluebonnets. These Odessans assume that Dan Rather captures the truth with his camera. They believe that the news reporter, who arrives at the accident and then submits his report to the copy editor who rearranges and adjusts his truth, objectively reports the news. And they cuss Martin Scorsese because, when he has the disciples speak with Brooklyn accents rather than the traditional Hollywood British and midwestern American accents, he violates the "facts" about Christ.

As concerns my points about art in the desert, maybe, the traditional arts no longer have the ability to persuade us as they could in the past. Today *Uncle Tom's Cabin* would have to be filmed before it could influence our populace. As a visually illiterate populace that nevertheless gets most of its information from TV, we are ripe for "documentaries" such as Leni Riefenstahl's *Triumph of the Will.* She "objectively" captured Hitler's Nuremberg rally and, in so doing, added thrill, drama, and political momentum to national socialism. It is time we all went to film grammar school.

And even though many Texans are writing about Texas and the play between myth and reality (not just Larry McMurtry and certainly not James Michener), too many Texans don't read. If they did, they would most likely be offended by what they read. They are too busy worrying about or escaping through TV or movies. Many Odessans confused *Lonesome Dove* with James Michener's *Texas.* But when *Lonesome Dove* came out on TV, it had a far more pronounced effect. While *Lonesome Dove* was being broadcast, the TV sets of devout Baptists were clicking as they changed their channels to CBN because of the crude language and subject matter in *Lonesome Dove.* Some devout professional conservatives in the Daughters of the Texas Revolution claimed that *Lonesome Dove* (the TV show only since they did not read the novel) did not present a true picture of our Texas forefathers.

Thus, we get into a real quagmire of different myths and realities. Perhaps for many Texans, Roy Rogers, John Wayne, and Louis L'Amour's heroes are reality. Other Odessans liked TV's *Lonesome Dove* because they found some sort of link with a myth; others disliked it because it took too long to get started (it was not like the fast-paced *Miami Vice*). For others it was just another TV show or movie and, therefore, nothing as important as the newscast or the nonfiction books that they don't read.

All the while some West Texans, in their jokes and stories, are fashioning the rudiments of myth and thus art. Their jokes and anecdotes are the equivalent of a poet's doodling.

While modern poetry may be dead, decadent, incestuous, or not, and while the masses and even a sizable bunch of intelligent minorities have rejected poetry, the basis for poetry still exists, and the masses still try to write or appreciate poetry even if crudely and rudimentarily in love poems, bluebonnet paintings, sentimental stories, and obituaries. Maybe their output comes to be drivel, but it is certainly better stuff than most TV, movies, and music because these are all commercial manipulation and little poetic impulse. The next step for these unsophisticated poets is to overcome their knee-jerk sentimentality. The key to Walt Disney's old movies, Texas poems about or paintings of the splendor of Texas or love, and pornography is excessive and/or easy emotion: puppy dogs, parting boyfriends, old coots, or large love equipment. Thus, like pornography, love poems and bluebonnet paintings use not earned sentiment but unearned emotion, or sentimentality.

Large numbers of students enroll in creative writing classes (even in West Texas), despite the fact that very few will become poets or writers, because these students feel the blood in their veins. They sense that their language, thoughts, and feelings are the basis of something profound or shared. They are aware, as Eluterio Garza became aware, of their need for poetry. A student in my sophomore literature class, Eluterio barely passed because someone neglected his writing skills, but after reading several twentieth-century poets, Eluterio informed me that, no matter what his grade, the "stories" we read made him feel that what he felt had been felt before, and that thus he could trust himself more. Eluterio, without a technical command of the language, may not become a poet or ever buy a collection of poems, but he can certainly feel and see poetry.

And without knowing it, Eluterio first experienced poetry when he heard or repeated the obscene jokes, the stories, the anecdotes of West Texas. The joke about the prostitute learning to play pool with a rope and T. Tyree's stories about the oil field in the forties and about his life with Mama reveal the human desire to know or to feel something beyond "self" that is yet contained in "self" and then to render this feeling or insight into words or some other "form." These people may not read poems, but they sense what poetry is.

Though he never liked his label as a storyteller or as a local colorist, Mark Twain put the anecdotes and stories of his boyhood, of Mississippi steamboating, and of California gold mining to good use. Flannery O'Connor and James Dickey must both have listened to people like T. Tyree and Pete Proctor tell their sexual and scatological anecdotes. O'Connor has her typical college-educated woman in "Good Country People," but she also uses her audience's knowledge of all the jokes about the traveling salesman and the farmer's daughter. She knows about our southerners' knowledge about Bible salesmen. During my freshman year in college, several recruiters showed up in the dorms and promised big bucks and free transportation to Alabama, Mississippi, and Tennessee in order to sell Bibles door to door. The greediest, the most desperate, the most loathsome, the most stupid, or the most gullible of my freshman friends signed up. Most got dumped in the rural South and came back without any money.

Our respective daddies must have told James Dickey and me about this man-goat embryo that "they got hid away." For me, it was at Texas A&M; for Dickey, it was at the big museum in Atlanta. Dickey finds further inspiration in Greek myth and in Yeats's "Leda and The Swan," but he uses that nasty old southern-boy myth as the basis for his harrowing poem "Sheep Child."

In my discussions with friends who are also colleagues, I may grow intellectual, or when I read some criticism or philosophy, I may grow sophisticated or intellectually "hip." But, whether moral relativists, Platonists, deconstructionists, phenomenologists, pragmatists, or existentialists, we are just more glib versions of T. Tyree and Eluterio Garza. Even if we denounce truth, we try to account for some feeling of truth. We may just intuit truth. But we hope to share this feeling. Thus, people write poems, sculpt, paint, write dissertations, attend academic conferences, get into discussions with colleagues, share a beer with Tyree and the boys, or listen to an old prostitute. I won't deny that in some of these activities racism, sexism, just plain ignorance, or other forms of prejudice show up. But wrongheaded prejudices are just an unfortunate by-product of the real impulse in these activities: a need for poetry.

The people who worry about the social damage that art might do are neurotics. They stymie poetry. Bureaucrats, administrators, legalists, and religionalists who are scared of the unfortunate by-products, as well as their own well-guarded psyches, all stymie art.

I want Eluterio to risk his job and some low grades to feel what Robert Frost felt and give himself some private satisfaction. I only secondarily worry about his public actions. His quandary is symptomatic of the confused yearnings and head butting of West Texas and perhaps of the country, of the public messages whispered to us and the suppressed shouting of our egos. And because of these yearnings, I think it is a sign of growing self-awareness that, though poetry is being read less and less, more and more people are wanting to write poetry—or short stories, or to paint, or to sculpt.

This yearning that West Texans feel, even if they don't develop it, is the antidote to a West Texas mentality that wants no complexity in myth, art, or history. If Texans would pay more attention to their confusion and to the bullshit coming from their bars and beauty parlors than to their blind faith in an unexamined past or socially appropriate version of that past, then Texas might become a more beautiful place to live.

Old Corrals

TEXAS ACCORDING TO 80S FILMS AND TV SHOWS AND TEXAS ACCORDING TO LARRY MCMURTRY

For fifteen years now, in conversations, at conventions, and at cocktail parties, I have noticed Texans arguing about Texas literature. The same arguments have appeared in print from the *Texas Monthly* to the *Texas Observer* to *The Concho River Review.* The more notorious of these articles raised literary dust across the state from the stamping feet of angered Texas critics and writers. Palefaces, Redskins, and bridegrooms all have different and sometimes conflicting notions about what a Texas writer is and what Texas writing is. The Texas Institute of Letters annually awards cash money to the best Texas literature. But, as Jim Lee says in *Range Wars,* neither the institute, the prize winners, nor observers can figure out its rules for eligibility. No one seems to know what qualifies someone to be a Texas writer, although Clay Reynolds does a good job in his essay in *Range Wars* (S.M.U. Press). Texas critics and writers may be copying the same phrase that so many West Texans say about art: They don't know how to define Texas literature, but they know what it is when they read it. Or so they think.

The same sort of mist surrounds most things Texan. Few Texans can even agree about what a Texan is: a native, a native moved away, a New Yorker with sympathies, a naturalized Texan like my father, who, nevertheless, after living in Texas nearly forty years claims not to be a Texan. To me, Texans seem, on the one hand, to have an overemphasized love and hate for their territory; yet they don't want anyone other than a Texan telling them about Texas. On the other hand, the nation as a whole has a certain fascination with Texas, perhaps for the same reasons that Texans love it and hate it—the cowboys (both wranglers and football players), rural poverty and oil wealth, tarball beaches and truly ugly West Texas emptiness. To the nation, Texas is an example of unrestrained Americanness, manifest destiny gone unchecked, Lyndon Johnson showing compassion by declaring war on poverty yet conducting an unpopular war from his toilet seat. I love to hate Lyndon because of his embarrassing crudity, but I hate to love him because of his naturalness compared to the tight-assed, Harvard-trained, Europeanized Kennedy men who surrounded him.

So to say anything about Texas, a critic or a bullshitter has to define whether he is talking about a national perception of Texas, Texans' perception of Texas, or some personal observations about Texas. I want to talk about, or bullshit about, art in Texas and artistic portrayals of Texas. In this chapter I'll address some national perceptions of Texas as presented by a television series, a film, and a novel. I'll leave other art out since I don't know much about it and don't want blatantly to reveal my ignorance.

Since TV is the most pervasive American art form (the term *art* is used here for lack of a better term), I'll discuss a TV show. Because film is the most popular and dominant medium of the twentieth century, perhaps the form for folk art in this century, I'll discuss movies about Texas. And, since he is a bright guy and an icon, I'll discuss Larry McMurtry with regard to a novel in which he wrestles with his identity as a Texas writer to a national audience.

MINOR MAINTENANCE OF THE TEXAS SPIRIT IN *THE YELLOW ROSE*

By 1983 the urban cowboy was dead. Though San Antonians, Houstonians, and Dallasites still dressed in shiny boots and hats and drove pickup trucks to cavernous dance halls, New Yorkers no longer wanted lizard-skin boots, and the young John Travolta was no longer marketable. But no sooner had the mechanical bulls grown rusty when the country was again ready to buy traditional notions about Texas.

In the summer of 1983 Robert Duvall appeared in his Academy Award–winning performance as a modern-day "rural" Texan in *Tender Mercies.* Max Sledge had been to Nashville, but by the start of the movie he is stranded at a culturally barren Texas outpost. The simplicity of life at Tess Harper's aging young lady's gas station/motel contrasts with Sledge's daughter's

(Ellen Barkin's) modern-day world of fast cars and an indulgent mother. His new life also provides him with the film's tender mercies. As was the case with *Lonesome Dove,* a Texan, Horton Foote, wrote the screenplay and an Australian, Bruce Beresford, directed. Why is it that Australian directors make incisive movies about Texans if guided by a Texas screenwriter? Two years later Foote got *The Trip to Bountiful* refilmed, and Geraldine Page joined Duvall and Gregory Peck *(To Kill a Mockingbird)* in winning an Academy Award from a Foote screenplay. But nobody really saw *The Trip to Bountiful,* and even fewer people saw *Valentine's Day* and *1918,* both Foote screenplays turned into movies in 1986.

More important as a barometer of national sentiment toward Texas, in 1983 executives at NBC were willing to gamble that Americans would watch a TV series about Texans. They were wrong, but their assumption is what counts. I first heard about the series when my mother, a part-time wardrobe lady, went to work with the crew at the Moody Ranch near Del Rio. Mom dreamed of glamorous, steady, well-paying employment through working on a TV series, but she worked just on the first episode. Later, to cut expenses, the series filmed in the southern California hills since, as the producers said, the two locales looked the same. Hollywood has always had a peculiar notion about what Texas looked liked. Mom also sneaked me a shooting script, and, through the script, I saw what the TV people had in mind.

Just before the TV series premiered with a lot of network ballyhoo, Mark Goodman, reviewing the then-new TV shows in *Family Weekly,* September 25, 1983, said that *The Yellow Rose* was "essentially *Dallas* in dusty boots." Goodman's remark indicated the calculated marketing of NBC's acceptance of *The Yellow Rose* as a series; NBC was betting the success of the series on the early 1980s popularity of soap operas such as *Dallas* and *Dynasty* and on the country's fascination with Texas. However, in 1983 the executive producers Michael Zinberg and John Wilder wanted to do more than remake *Dallas.* They wanted something more honest, like *Tender Mercies.* As Zinberg said prior to the opening of the series, "Texas has a mystique about it. There is a sense of heritage, a source of personal strength. Room for individuals and pioneers. We found people in Texas who are cutting their own paths in a very complicated world. Texas was a frontier, a place where the brightest men and women could go out and cut their own fortune" (as quoted by Bob Stewart, "TV Week," *San Antonio Light,* October 2, 1983, p. T4). The San Antonio newspapers ate up the network's promotions. Zinberg, a San Antonio native who went to Jefferson High, may be correct in his metaphorical implications about pioneers and a frontier. But he certainly is far away from the literal with his remarks about the best and brightest going to the frontier. Apparently, from the comment, *The Yellow Rose* would deal only with metaphor or myth.

At first, early in 1983, before the series received dismal ratings, Zinberg gave concessions to marketable melodrama in the format and plots, but he maintained a setting and characters that showed his interest in Texas as myth and its modern-day relevance. Zinberg first conceived of the series in order to promote south Texas, to show a "real" Texas, and to pay homage to the Old West. Zinberg, following the guidance of J. Frank Dobie, saw Texas as a part of the West, not as an extension of the South or even of Mexico.

Zinberg sought out John Wilder, the writer and producer of the twenty-six-hour *Centennial,* hoping that Wilder would be able to translate both their interests in the West into a script for a TV pilot. Wilder had problems with the network and walked away from the project. After the series started, Zinberg also had problems with the network and walked away from the series. Story editor David Abramowitz saw Zinberg's intention to show a "real" and modern Texas while paying homage to a mythic Texas as the basis for the major conflict in the series. I eventually talked to Abramowitz, who spoke about Texas with a New York accent.

Wilder's script for the pilot, the resulting first episode of the series, is a classy soap opera for commercial reasons but established the tensions between a mythic Texas and a modern, real Texas. Abramowitz told me over the phone that the theme of the series lies in the characters' conflicts with the "reconciliation of the old and the New West" and with the "maintenance of the spirit of the Old West in the modern West." Surprisingly, the script for the pilot and the first few episodes, while paying homage to the western heritage, showed some of that heritage's destructive elements in the main characters and thus distinguished the series from most syrupy TV shows.

Two supporting characters embodied the value and the reality of the myth and thus the nostalgia in the series. Coryell and Dillard were a pair of sidekicks, sort of a comedy team of Andy Devine and Walter Brennan. In casting against type, the producers had Noah Berry play the comedian to Ken Curtis's straight man. Both actors were veteran sidekicks, Berry having supported James Garner in *The Rockford Files* and Ken Curtis having supported James Arness in *Gunsmoke.* Abramowitz meant for them to be relics from the past, physical remnants of the Old West, the 1880s lost in the 1980s. They were supposed to look as near to nineteenth-century cowboys as possible:

> *Luther Dillard and Hoyt Coryell are a little older now, a little slower than they were in their prime. But, then, they were never in that big a hurry anyway. And, although they may have moved easier then, rode straighter, they were never more proud. Theirs is the justifiable pride of the survivor. It is etched deeply into leathered faces that have been toughened for nearly three quarters of a century by the relentless sun that hammers down from that cloudless West Texas sky. The direct link to another time when any man worth his salt was always true to his work, and a sense of humor was all a man really had to balance the scales that seemed to, forever, be tipping against him. (script, scene 14, p. 5)*

Abramowitz said that, in the scenes that they have together, they were to "offer moments of the Old West that can not be advanced through story or plot," and that they were to function as a "Greek chorus, commenting upon plot and character from a traditional standpoint." That Greek-chorus comparison first seemed ludicrous to me, but then it showed that some literate, thoughtful people were working in Hollywood. What is a Greek chorus but a bunch of old men gathered at the Dairy Queen gossiping or bullshitting? My estimation of Hollywood folks went up. Maybe too many thoughtful people, and some wishful thinkers, fouled this series.

The landscape also added tremendously to the premiere's western atmosphere. As I mentioned, the first episode was filmed near Del Rio. As Chance, the lead, steps off a bus and squints at the land in the opening scene, we see the integration of character and environment and the effect of the land on the character that the script suggested:

> *This is the land the Mexicans called the monte, the Brasada. A land known to the Texans as the Brush Country, an ungracious, hostile host that jabs its way south from Del Rio and San Antonio toward the Rio Grande and the Mexican*

Border. A land which the cat's claw, Spanish dagger, white brush, and black chaparral stand guard over a reckless wasteland where soldiers have suffered, missionaries have died, vaqueros have ranched, outlaws have sought refuge . . . and where the American Cowboy created an important industry with the greatest cattle herds on the face of the earth. (scene 6, pp. 2–3)

In the outdoor settings of the pilot the wind blows, cows bellow, the sun shines brightly. The landscapes have have a red or brown hue, evoking a rustic, antique look. There is none of the staginess of back lots or of all-purpose landscapes around Los Angeles. The authentic architecture—the ranch house, the chuckwagon/house trailer of Grace Mckenzie—seen surrounded by the rugged Texas landscape expresses the ranchers' uneasy truce with nature and sometimes absurd-looking meetings of landscape and man-made structures. At its best, the series resembled a miniature, TV-size version of *Giant* through its use of landscape to enhance its conflict between the Old and New West. Zinberg regretted the move to California: "We would like to shoot in Texas. The land is very much a character in the piece. But, we can't do it yet" (as quoted by Bob Stewart, "TV Week," *San Antonio Light,* October 2, 1983, p. T4). Abramowitz believed that the shift to California would not cause problems, since California has a variety of scenery. Apparently, he had never seen Del Rio. The rest of the series did not look like the first episode.

In the first few episodes the lead characters find conflict in the nostalgia that Coryell and Dillard and the landscape establish. Chance is the spirit of the Old West trying to survive in the modern world. Abramowitz explained that Chance believes in the agrarian ideal and embodies the typical conflict in Westerns: the lone individual trying to exist in a homogeneous society. His name was not meant to be so much a macho label as a description of his precarious position in the world. Abramowitz described him as a "tough man, who, when he speaks, speaks with a mythic eloquence in few words. He is not to be trifled with." The pace of the pilot's script gives Chance many highlighted short speeches with precise and often salient dialogue. In the screen directions the script reveals what Chance meant to the makers of the series:

CLOSE ON THE MAN

FROM LOW ANGLE, adding to the sense of mystery about him. And to see what he wears, the stylish, working wardrobe of a contemporary American Cowboy. His boots are as dusty, and his jeans and shirt as faded, as his Stetson. A wide belt with a big buckle circles his trim waist. He is tall angular, with powerful, sloping shoulders, deeply tanned skin. He is cut from the same mold as the legendary adventurers that drove the great Longhorn steers up the lonely trails to Kansas and Colorado. There is an immediately identifiable independence about him that is the essence of that rare breed who became a cornerstone of America's concept of itself. He stands rooted in a place a moment longer, his keen, hawk-like gaze drifting over

THE RANGE LAND — POINT OF VIEW

This is the land the Mexicans called the Monte, the Brasada. A land known to the Texans as the Brush Country . . .

CLOSE ON THE MAN

as he takes in this vast, jagged landscape that possesses such dreadful beauty. This place where the low-slung mesquite is the only tree tough enough, defiant enough, strong enough to fight its way through the sun drenched, rain-starved soil. And his lips release a small, private smile. Perhaps, because he is reminded that the mesquite gives no shade, no shelter, no relief from scorching sun and blast furnace winds. Because he understands that when there is no shade under which a man can sit, he learns to stand tall. This is a tall man. A man called CHANCE. (scenes 7–9, pp. 2–3)

As with all screen directions, these were written for an actor's understanding, not for subtlety or nuance. Actors must be particularly dull witted and sentimental, since these directions seem to drip off the page. The scene comes off better on-screen. Chance is not so much a caricature, and the impact is much more subtle because the producers were lucky enough to get Sam Elliot to play Chance. According to Abramowitz, Elliot is the "quintessential Western hero." He looks like a John Wayne, Gary Cooper, Henry Fonda, or James Arness. Both Abramowitz and Elliot realized that he has a screen presence that seems to demand a Western role (unfortunately for Elliot, the 1970s and 1980s had few Western roles). From his first film, *Lifeguard,* through his TV movies, Elliot has played characters like Chance who are not quite at ease in their environments. Elliot said in interviews that he accepted the part because the series was authentic and because Chance was a real, working cowboy: "The one concern I have with this character is that he not become an urban cowboy. That he remain a working cowboy. By doing that I can stay true personally to that affinity I have for making westerns" (as portrayed by Leona Pappas, "TV Now," *San Antonio Express and News,* October 2, 1983, pp. 3, 4, 5).

Unlike Chance, Roy, Chance's half brother, is a modern westerner. He has adapted better than Chance to modern ranch life—financing, drilling, and flying as well as riding and roping. If Chance must learn how to exist in a modern world, Roy must learn how to mingle the disparate parts of his character: the psychological dependence on the Old West and the New West practicality of managing The Yellow Rose Ranch. Roy inherited both his psychological dependence and his managerial job from his father. Because Roy is more complex than Chance, Wilder spends more time describing him in screen directions. Roy first appears in the script in the cockpit of a Cessna. On-screen we first see the spinning rotors of the Cessna, then Roy in the cockpit. He is clearly modern. He is at "the helm of whatever it is that needs steering," the script says (Wilder, scene 31, p. 29). Furthermore, in the script Wilder notes that Roy is dressed in a modern fashion, coat and tie, but he wears a western suit and cowboy hat. He is tough but haunted: "And will take very little more from any man now. Because the man from whom he took so much is gone, there is no real resolution for many of Roy Champion's problems. He loved his father deeply, but not blindly. Because he knew the man in ways Wade Champion never let any other person know him. And because he never felt the love he saw his father lavish on others" (Wilder, scene 33, p. 29).

The pressure of managing the ranch and his memory of his father—that strain of the Old West that is reactionary, nonchanging, and aloof—make him volatile, at times manic, but admirable:

> *All work and no play. . . . That has been Roy Champion's existence for a long, long time. . . . It makes him a man, about whom there is an ever present sense of danger. And if bridling direct action is the most difficult thing that can be asked of him, breaking a trust is impossible. . . . If you want his friendship, you'll have to beat him at something hard. And you'll have to play the game the way he does. Hard. And fair. . . . The only person Roy Champion finds it impossible to forgive for being afraid is himself. And the only fear he knows is the loss of that which defines his existence (The Yellow Rose ranch). (scene 33, p. 30)*

David Soul was cast, not only for his acting but because, as Abramowitz said, "he looks modern." Viewers would remember him from *Starsky and Hutch,* a modern series. As Abramowitz said, he was able to look the part of the Old West as well as the New.

Roy, then, must exorcise the destructive parts of his memory of his father and learn how to adapt the spirit of the Old West to the New West. Chance must, in classic western fashion, preserve his identity in a hostile, changing environment. With these two characters existing in the same series, their inevitable collisions, confrontations, and reconciliations create much of the drama. The first episode ends with an uneasy alliance between the two New West archetypes.

Furthermore, the old power and spirit of the West, Wade Champion, psychologically scars Chance and Roy and interferes with their respective sexual and familial relations with Colleen, Wade's twenty-nine-year-old widow (she and Wade married when she was nineteen and he was sixty-five). Though he is dead, Wade pervades the series through a portrait—especially commissioned to resemble Elliot and Soul—hung in the ranch house living room. In the script and the first episode, we follow Roy into the living room to see the portrait: "The focal point in the room is a large, oil painting of Wade Champion. The room is much warmer than the face in the painting. But it is an attractive face, a strong face, and Roy communes silently with it as he sips an amber-colored drink" (scene 64, p. 46). The portrait becomes a symbol of the dominance of Wade. The characters consort beneath it while Daddy watches. When I asked about it, Abramowitz said he hoped that eventually "Chance and Colleen [Roy too, I suspect] would burn it." To Abramowitz, it represented the unconditional, nonchanging, out-of-place, and thus incomplete side of the Old West. Chance, Roy, and Colleen would never come to terms with themselves or each other until they overcome the dominance of Wade. In fact, the series veered off into melodrama and then abruptly ended before the main characters could ever make a campfire with Daddy's portrait.

With the hair-trigger psyches of Chance and Roy and the intrusive portrait of Wade, *The Yellow Rose* became rather schizophrenic in its attitudes about Texas's western heritage. The poetic/mythic part of Chance's nature and his appearance, the opening of the series in later episodes with Remingtonesque paintings and a duet of the ballad "The Yellow Rose of Texas," and the antics and comments of Coryell and Dillard made the series nostalgic, made the past a better time. But the crippling effects of the myth on Roy's and Chance's emotional and psychological equilibrium showed the myth as an intrusive residue in the minds of modern Texans. So despite what fondness it has for a mythic Texas, *The Yellow Rose*'s nostalgia had an edge; it was not always pleasant—and the present was not always worse than the past.

With a social and political consciousness of modern Texas, the producers created two characters who were modern Texans, who weren't haunted by the past or belonged to it. Colleen and Quisto would not have had star billing in previous Westerns. Quisto, another half brother, is half Mexican. He is a lawyer who dresses, when he is off the ranch, as Roy does, in western-style suits. He is outspoken in his defense of and attitudes about Texans, Mexicans, and their relations. Most important, he is not a Hollywood stereotype. As played by a tanned Edward Albert, Quisto is a shrewd politician and manager with an easy-going manner: "Quisto brings to the series a Western heritage that predates the Anglo West and the modern Western reality of the Hispanic's new-found influence. He, more so than Roy, is able to blend the old and the new, taking the resources from each as he needs them."

Colleen, Wade's young widow (Cybill Shepherd), manages the stock and the breeding on The Yellow Rose. Surely some TV executives giggled and licked their chops at pre-*Moonlighting* Cybill watching copulating horses. Abramowitz planned to have her take a more active part in all aspects of managing the ranch in successive episodes (again, though, NBC canceled the series). The assertive female, she also makes the first advances toward Chance. Of course, Colleen also makes advances toward Roy so that Cybill Shepherd, in tight jeans rather than designer dresses, is in charge of *all* the breeding in the series.

Quisto and Colleen represent the new power in the West, the new westerners who are gaining some of the political power and financial clout. As the series developed, Colleen and Quisto, living in the present and for the future, appreciated the past but didn't long for it or let it interfere with their well-being.

One other character, Grace Mckenzie, the Champions' cook and handywoman, is an attempt at defining a world-weary, ill-fated West Texas woman: "The woman on the porch is even more handsome at a second glance. The slow smile seems to land directly below the belt. And what lies beneath her own belted housedress is equally provocative as she moves across the porch and enters the house with a feline grace that defines every movement, every gesture of this warm, if weary, woman called Grace Mckenzie" (Wilder, scene 14, p. 4). Susan Anspach, giving the best performance in the series, makes the sparsely developed character with the sparsely covered genitalia into a lonely woman on the verge of desperation, holding on to herself through stoicism and wit. With the few hints in the script, Anspach creates a character full of the nuances and scars of place and time. Grace, even if an attempt at injecting sex into the series, seems the most authentic West Texan (however, Anspach, a free spirit, soon quit the series).

Finally, *The Yellow Rose* reserved most of its plots for soap opera, through what Abramowitz called "interpersonal relationships," through Byzantine complexities reminiscent of other TV serials. As in the other TV soap operas, women provided the sex, and villains (here Chuck Connors as Hollister) provided an external, easily identifiable conflict. But, at least through the first several episodes, the discerning viewer could see the more interesting internal conflicts etched out by the actors. For Wilder, Zinberg, and Abramowitz saw in the characters, and to a lesser degree in the composition of the series, the conflict of balancing the spirit of the Old West (a spirit that may never have existed in the nineteenth century and is more of twentieth-century nostalgia) against the practicality and the realities of the modern West. Primarily through Wilder's and Abramowitz's guidance, *The Yellow Rose* became another screen version of Texas nostalgia. Their contribution to this subgenre was to show the conflict that a fond, mythic past can create in the modern Texan. They tried to show the effect of a Texas heritage and myth on present Texas society. Unfortunately, Michael Zinberg quit the series after a disagreement with NBC executives about the story line. His original concept was destroyed. Ultimately, the series was canceled. The pervasive soft-core melodrama that TV producers equate with drama and TV audiences accept as entertainment defeated the portrayal of our loosening connections with a mythic past.

In retrospect, though, I think that Zinberg got lost from the beginning. Unraveling myth and reality and then trying to sort out whose myth and whose reality have destroyed the intents of a lot of honest Texas work. Zinberg, an urban Texan from San Antonio, like his characters, got lost among a real, urban Texas, an old frontier Texas, a national myth about cowboys, and slick TV melodrama. After Zinberg failed, Robert Benton did better with nostalgia, myth, and reality; and Larry McMurtry seems to have the firmest and most subtle control.

TEXAS NOSTALGIA IN *PLACES IN THE HEART*

As evidenced by *The Yellow Rose* and *Tender Mercies* and the repeated film tampering with Texas, Texas seems to be a ripe locale for what John Cawelti calls nostalgic films. Cawelti describes the transformation of film genres (Westerns, detective films, musicals, etc.) that "are no longer fully adequate to the imaginative needs of our time" into new film genres that are "more directly related to the imaginative landscape of the second half of the twentieth century" ("*Chinatown* and Generic Transformation In Recent American Films," 1979. *Film Theory and Criticism,* eds. Gerald Mast and Marshall Cohen, 3rd ed. New York: Oxford University Press, 1985. p. 520). He identifies "nostalgia" as one of the new genres. The nostalgia genre looks at the past through some modern context:

> *In this mode, traditional generic features of plot, character, setting and style are deployed to recreate the aura of a past time. The power of nostalgia lies especially in its capacity to evoke a sense of warm reassurance by bringing before our mind's eye images from a time when things seemed more secure and full of promise and possibility. . . . a contemporary nostalgic film cannot simply duplicate the past experience, but must make us aware in some fashion of the relationship between past and present. (514)*

In 1984, an election year in which we voted into office a president and senators of both parties who called to mind, sometimes incessantly, past American values, Hollywood staked a lot of money and stars staked their reputations on a triumvirate of nostalgia films. With the farmer being economically depressed but stirring old American agrarian notions about the sanctity and purity of farm life, many of these nostalgia films were about the plight of American farmers: for example, *The River, Country,* and *Places in the Heart.* The best of this lot was *Places in the Heart.*

Director and writer Robert Benton, a native of Waxahachie, is more specifically concerned with a nostalgic Texas. His screenplay for *Bonnie and Clyde* may have been the basis for a cinematic anthem for the 1960s, but the film was also about a distant, populist Texas. *Places in the Heart,* under Benton's guidance, rejects the westernness in Texas and instead looks at its southernness, and in this movie Yankees could see what much of Texas really looks like. *Places in the Heart* uses a nostalgic (and melodramatic) past to show, as Robert Benton says, "a sense of being in a place and part of a place that goes back further than anyone you know" (as quoted by Richard Schickel, "A Search for Connections," *Time,* September 24, 1984, p. 70). With Benton's assertive, almost feminist heroine (Sally Field), his racial commentary, the now-lost sense of place and slow-moving time that create bonds between humans, and the spirituality and transcendence that Benton finds at the end of the film to connect past and present, *Places in the Heart* makes us aware of a relationship between past and present.

In the simplistic, almost cornball story in *Places in the Heart* honesty, integrity, nobility, and courage oppose sneakiness, miserliness, pettiness, and prejudice. But the point of the film—its theme, its own honesty and integrity, its spirituality—is not in its story. These qualities are in the images. As Andre Bazin says in "Theater and Cinema," the "Decor" or the "architecture" of a film gives it its distinction. The "look" of a film makes it what it is as much as its story or characters (from *What Is Cinema,* rpt. in *Film Theory and Criticism,* eds. Gerald Mast and Marshall Cohen, 3rd ed. New York: Oxford University Press, 1985, pp. 360–66). Through the "decor," the look of the images and their juxtaposition in *Places in the Heart,* director Benton, cinematographer Nestor Almendros, and editor Carol Littleton extol the icons, traditions, and values that create a sense of community and place.

In the opening moments of the film, after Edna Spalding's (Sally Field's) sheriff husband, Royce, has been accidentally killed by a young, drunken black man, Benton and Littleton alternate images of blacks and whites in 1935 Waxahachie, Texas. First, friends of the slain sheriff bring the body home to Edna and display it on the dining room table. The local rednecks then drag the body of the black man behind a truck. Then, Benton and Littleton show us the funeral of the black man and the wonderfully sensual wake of the white man. Throughout we hear the hymns of the blacks and the whites. The two people are separate and unequal. Prejudice and unfairness exist along with economic misery in the 1930s. However, each group has a strong, cohesive sense of identity and community. Through the traditions, the customs, the icons—bringing the bodies home, the hymns, the chocolate cake at the wake—the two communities cohere and survive. The film, through similar cohesive images, confirms this point.

In carefully decorated scenes Benton dresses his characters and the setting. Edna visits her sister Margaret (Lindsay Crouse) shortly after Royce's death. While they chat in Margaret's living room, which she uses as a beauty parlor, Almendros's camera catches the fact that Edna's collar and Margaret's apron and drapes have similar flowered prints. These two women are sisters, live in the same town, and have the same ideas about family. These flowered prints reveal the strength and pervasiveness of the sisters' sense of themselves and their values. Both will have their communal and self-identities tested.

Benton goes on to sprinkle brief images and sounds throughout the film to enhance further the bindings of time and place. Repeatedly characters gather at and Benton shows cultural icons: the church, the courthouse, the dances, the cotton gin. Several times in the film Benton uses a montage of church, courthouse, and cotton gin in sequence to indicate the ruling trinity of the town. The sound track is filled with hymns and an intrusive train whistle that sounds through every crucial scene. Characters and photographs in the film refer to the cotton gins and cotton picking. These institutions and the customs that they create may be oppressive or manipulative—the blacks are treated as inferiors; the gin operator is a tyrant; cotton farming is a backbreaking task—but these commonalities bind these people, creating places in their hearts. And these images bind the film.

In a cotton-picking sequence Almendros finds angles, shots, and colors to show the power and influence of the land. In these scenes, which are reminiscent of Almendros's work in *Days of Heaven,* insects constantly whir, the sun is a constant irritant, and fingers bleed. In one zoom shot Almendros pulls from the characters to the immense thirty-acre field, thus making the characters' task tremendous and the land awesome. In one shot that has no Norman Rockwell cuteness but all the bluntness of reality, Almendros shows Edna's daughter sleeping in a wagon of freshly picked cotton. The landscape has no purple majesty, no inherent nobility (just like Texas's landscapes). As Almendros and Benton present it, it is mechanistic and indifferent to humans, thus creating a stark, naturalistic beauty.

Benton and his actors enhance this thematic stance in several poignant scenes and create the film's sense of loss. In a silent moment during a gin game, Margaret's husband (Ed Harris) and his lover (Amy Madigan) reveal their adulterous relationship to Margaret. In this world where tradition and community are vital, adultery threatens familial and thus other traditions. The two lovers are in danger of externalizing themselves from community and family. After this scene Margaret's husband tries diligently to ease back into his family and avoid catastrophe. His lover leaves town.

Edna, in trying to preserve her family, takes in a blind boarder, Will (John Malkovich), and houses a black beggar, Moze (Danny Glover), to help her bring in a cotton crop. These characters form their own community. With Sally Field doing her *Norma Rae* number (you really do like Sally Field), Edna tells Will and Moze of the tragic consequences of not bringing in the cotton crop: Will could go to the state hospital, and Moze would go back to begging. Being forced out of the group, disfranchisement, is the greatest tragedy. Accordingly, John Malkovich develops Will from a bitter individual to a courageous and contented member of Edna's extended family. Moze, after the KKK forces him off Edna's farm, becomes tragic because he suffers the film's most tragic fate: disfranchisement, expulsion from the family and the community.

In the final scene, which will probably become a film legend, Benton places his cast in church taking communion. He slowly pans across the pews to show all of his characters. We see Moze, whom we assume is long gone; then we see Edna's husband, Royce, and the black boy who shot him. Benton suggests the power of forgiveness. And, through the revelations and resolutions that his panning camera reveals, Benton lifts the film from reality into spirituality. The prejudice, the economic misery, the adultery, and the labor, as deplorable as they all are, create bonds and finally develop the characters' ability to transcend.

Places in the Heart, like *Tender Mercies,* is honest and well executed, an obvious work from the heart. But, like *Country* and *The River,* it seems one-sided; it leans toward neurosis. All three films, I think, are filmmakers' attempts to cash in on the Reagan patriotism in the country. They resurrect a populist mentality reminiscent of the 1930s and 1940s. The populism of the time and even the populist films of that time, though, had something of an edge to them.

Social dramas of the thirties and forties were angry. Ford, Capra, Welles, and Wilder all looked at individuals doomed by their own populist nature and by their opposition to society. *Country,* under Jessica Lange's guidance, has a tidy social message instead of a theme, and *The River* insists on deserting the plight of the individual to become populist and sentimental. *Places in the Heart,* to its credit, reminded me of John Ford's films, but while it examined the value of community and society, it neglected the inevitable conflict between the community and the individual that Ford always portrayed.

I saw Ford's *Young Cassidy* a day after seeing *Places in the Heart.* Though *Young Cassidy* is overly romantic and presents a simplification of the artist's motivations, it is more thematically ambitious than *Places.* Cassidy (based on Sean O'Casey), an Irishman devoted to family and community, loses friends and a lover when he honestly portrays his community onstage. Dublin ostracizes him. Yet it is not a complete defeat, for in leaving behind his community, he asserts his individuality and achieves his artistic potential. In his better films—*The Searchers, The Grapes of Wrath, How Green Was My Valley*—Ford's characters constantly struggle between self and community, and in the inevitable choice between the two, these characters might gain something—mythic stature, artistic achievement, independence, etc.—but suffer a bittersweet loss. In turn, society uses them, then completely consumes them or throws them away. And to complicate Ford's myths further, his individuals aren't so admirable. Ethan Edwards and Tom Joad are kin to Liberty Valance; all are sadistic psychopaths. And Jimmy Stewart's Fordian heroes are all glad-handing neurotics.

Thus, Ford—in working with nostalgia—made the memory and fondness of the past the conflict itself (as *The Yellow Rose* attempted to do). As his films progressed, we were aware of the present, for better or worse, always creeping into the nostalgic past and destroying it and its characters. Ultimately, the apolitical Ford was more honest about the past than the present conservatives.

Places in the Heart is a very good film, certainly the best of the eighties farm films, an impressive example of craft and integrity. In a way, though, this film is like the rebellious sixties films that rapidly become dated because they stressed self over the community. The theme of *Places in the Heart* is more appropriate for a conservative time. As a gauge of national temperament, it shows a national interest in Texas. For, despite or in addition to the urban Texas of Dallas (the TV show, the Republican Convention, the Cowboys), Americans see a nostalgic potential in Texas. We associate Texas with the past, its rural roots. Even in *Dallas* and in Dallas, people wear cowboy boots and western hats. Americans and Texans themselves see the state more as a myth than a reality, perhaps as a patriotic, traditional, conservative paradise, qualities that always seemed present in a nostalgic past. Larry McMurtry is a tougher wrestler. He tries harder to pin myth and nostalgia.

NUZZLING THE CORRAL IN *ANYTHING FOR BILLY*

With his early successes, *Horseman Pass By* and *Leaving Cheyenne,* Larry McMurtry, perched up on the corral post in the dust jacket photo, saw the God of national acclaim and popular success. With the first movies—*Hud* and *The Last Picture Show*—and then with Academy Awards raining down upon *Terms of Endearment,* McMurtry was nominated for beatification. Then with the Pulitzer Prize for *Lonesome Dove* and the following media event, the film version of *Lonesome Dove,*—*the* TV event of the 1988–89 season—McMurtry achieved popular sainthood. As a result, no Texan discussing literature or Texas dare leave him out. But as soon as any critic mentions McMurtry, Texas readers sigh and groan. For, because of Archer City's golden boy, Texans can't talk about Texas without talking about McMurtry.

I don't mean to imply that *Lonesome Dove* is not a good novel or TV show. McMurtry and his TV translators know about the cultural baggage in Americans' minds. Though bounded by the small screen that barely contains the livestock or the story, the miniseries has a visual and thematic complexity rarely seen from a living room sofa. Director Simon Wincer understands open space and cattle, and he films them both well; and Austin writer Bill Wittliff knows about playing realism against myth (again, what is it about Texan/Australian writer/director teams?).

So in *Lonesome Dove* a viewer sees the aching realism of the desperately psychologically and materialistically impoverished nineteenth-century Texas yet senses the mythic proportions in the physical and mental struggles in the film. Robert Duvall understands this tone and perhaps even Texas. As Gus McCrae and as the down-and-out country-western singer, Max Sledge, in *Tender Mercies* (a historical descendant but cinematic predecessor of Woodrow Call), Duvall shows the potential greatness in the moves, the physiques, and the voices of his Texan characters (not that native Texan Tommy Lee Jones doesn't sit a horse and the role rather nicely, but wouldn't it have been something to see Duvall play both leads in *Lonesome*

Dove?). Gus's movements show a primitive, untrained, and impulsive showboater. Gus's crudity and savagery (slamming a bartender's nose into the bar for not recognizing him and for calling him an old man) enable him to survive; yet his attempts at grandiose rhetoric, deeds, thought, and movement show the real becoming myth. Duvall gets the tone just right, but he got the idea for that tone from McMurtry's novel.

The miniseries, though, had some inevitable problems with its audience. My mother, who hasn't been in a movie theater in twenty-five years and who had a TV diet of *Dallas* and *Dynasty,* offered what I thought to be the best criticism of the TV special. They mixed the modern with the old-timey, my mother said, specifically when they had the cattle's horns light up and in some other places that she couldn't remember. What my mother meant was that static electricity radiating around the longhorns' horns may have been historically accurate, but to a TV audience conditioned to special effects, the film presentation seemed too modern, as though it belonged in a *Star Wars* sequel. The special-effecty overtook the old-timey.

Maybe my mother's comment indicates that the rendering of the West on film is indeed dead. The technology of filming and audiences' expectations about what modern film wizardry can record does not include the Western. We can have films about pre-Dark Age barbarians, which become in the film world somehow displaced in time, but not about Westerns, because Westerns have to be filmed with old-timey fortyish and fiftyish film techniques. This expectation has nothing to do with history but only with myth. Even with *Lonesome Dove*'s high ratings, TV producers and moviemakers may not be able to find new explorations of the nineteenth-century West that escape the audience's notions about how the nineteenth-century West should look on film. The West or Texas as part of western myth, then, is probably best presented so that the audience can't *see* it. McMurtry has readers and not viewers and thus doesn't have to deal with film apprehensions. But even with print, he has to deal with his audiences' mythic apprehensions. He is, in the eyes of the country and even in the eyes of grouchy Texas critics, "a Texas writer" (who uses the term on what occasion determines whether it is derogatory or not).

Larry is now so closely associated with Texas that each time he picks up a pen or presses his fingers to any of his portable typewriters, he simultaneously comments about Texas, the country's ideas about Texas, and the ideas about Texas that he created. And because he has become such a literary brand name, each time he writes, he displays his own talents and habits and bumps against the scarred wooden posts of the literary corral that surrounds him. His fame and accompanying money and his own interests and instincts have brought him the freedom to dedicate himself to developing his craft yet put limits around what form that craft will take.

So readers, mostly those who buy a novel to enjoy it rather than to critique it, fully expect to jump off the fence post into McMurtry's corral when they fold back the spine of any recent McMurtry novel. After the Pulitzer, after *Texasville,* while *Lonesome Dove* was on the screen, readers were turning the pages of *Anything for Billy,* in which McMurtry perhaps consciously looks at his own dilemma. And as reader and potential reviewer or commentator, I too am stuck in his corral.

McMurtry is primarily a realist. Not Barthelme or Barth, he is concerned with what he wishes his text to show rather than with the text itself. But he at times becomes enamored of his text and pushes it far away from the worldly pastures where he starts. This tendency represents McMurtry at his worst and his best.

When he stays with his realism, he presents an ironic and laconic world and revels in its ordinariness and normalcy. He makes boredom, whether high-plains travel or small-town West Texas life, seem funny, touching, or pathetic. McMurtry's simple heroes aren't blessed with much introspection, so they never develop much self-awareness. Their own peculiar natures are intriguing to them and us because they never seem able to control themselves or understand themselves. They are caught between neurosis and psychopathy (Gus is McMurtry's freest character and most rounded psychopath and so is not like these characters. Call is like them). McMurtry is at his best with these characters, and with them he stands firmly in the center of his corral. These types of characters exhibit McMurtry's strength.

In *Anything for Billy* as with *Lonesome Dove,* this myopic examination of the ordinariness behind the mythic proportions of the West or Texas accounts for the fascination in the novels. Like the slow-motion world at Lonesome Dove, the dreary, dirty world at Greasy Corners in New Mexico presents the figures we assume to be myth in their premythic days. The gunfighters and buffalo hunters gathered at Greasy Corners in *Anything for Billy* are a bunch of heroes who are cognizant of their reputations but trapped by their own simpleness and the grittiness of their milieu. These characters thus develop an ironic and cruel acceptance of death. McMurtry's point is that this ironic view, hiding a barrelful of insecurities and irritated by a simple mind and hostile environment, sometimes looks heroic and can, with the right coloring, escalate into myth.

But the myths, as Ben Sippy (McMurtry's narrator) observes, can never stand in for the specific characteristics of those "sweethearts" at Greasy Corners:

> *The dime novelists might portray gunfighters as a confident, satisfied lot — I've been guilty of that myself — but the truth is they were mainly disappointed men. They spent their lives in the rough barrooms of ugly towns; they ate terrible food and drank a vile grade of liquor; few of them managed to shoot the right people, and even fewer got to die gloriously in a shoot-out with a peer. The majority just got shot down by some bold stranger, like the drunk who killed the great Hickok.*

McMurtry is at his traditional best in *Anything for Billy* when he positions his narrator in space and time to observe a shooting contest between Katerina Garza and legendary gunfighter Hill Coe. Katerina Garza, like many of McMurtry's women, has the self-assurance and conviction that his males so often lack. Even McMurtry's narrator cannot quite figure out Katerina and is awed by the other female characters, including his own wife. Katerina squats, takes careful aim, and shoots twenty bottles in a row. Next, Hill Coe will shoot his twenty. He misses the first one. Embarrassed and disgraced, Hill falls into a whiskey bottle. Billy, the famous outlaw, then tries his hand and hits only two of the twenty. The Yankee narrator, who is seen as something of an ineffectual oaf in the West, nearly matches Katerina's markswomanship. The tone of this scene—the manner in which McMurtry, while letting his narrator revel, downplays the skill and what we know about who will become myth and who will not—reveals McMurtry with his feet firmly planted in reality yet achingly dealing with a contrary myth.

But with some of his characters—Mesty-Woolah, Will Isinglass, and Lady Cecily Snow—McMurtry exhibits his weakness. I grew tired of Isinglass (John Chisum) and Snow, and Mesty-Woolah, and Wind Hill's castle. Too much seems exaggerated. McMurtry grows too extravagant. The trappings and architecture of Will Isinglass's ranch house, a castlelike creation; Will Isinglass's sexual appetites at age eighty-five; Lady Cecily Snow's icy and deadly character and expertise in botany; Mesty-Woolah's deadliness and red camel—all seem like characters from Ben Sippy's imagination rather than from his observation. And as all the characters converge at once to observe Billy Bone's death, McMurtry seems to give in to Sippy's sense of melodrama. I don't think that McMurtry is so much making a point here as just having fun. He deserts his narrative and simple sweetheart gunfighters to spend far too many pages lounging around with Sippy and these extravagant characters. They stop the novel and stomp the delicate play between the ordinariness and simplicity of the characters and their future mythic proportions.

I have heard McMurtry say that he writes for character and not plot. In the best realistic tradition, he lets his characters lead his plot wherever it might go. Ironically, though, McMurtry's fondness for his extravagant characters (perhaps the creations that earned his literary and commercial success) leads his novels away from their realistic tone. It is as though, with his characters, he tries to jump out of the world that he observes and into some world of his creation. But McMurtry can't jump as high as the magical realists. He sometimes ends up creating his own stereotypes. He spends perhaps needless pages describing these characters being characters. I put down *Terms of Endearment* several times because I got tired of Aurora Greenway and General Scot being eccentric. My first McMurtry book, *All My Friends Are Going To Be Strangers,* introduced me to this tendency when I read about Prof. Godwin Lloyd Jons, while naked, hanging on to the bumper of a coed's car. I was amused but didn't know what purpose these characters and their scenes served.

McMurtry along with these characters and the scenes that they force him to write seem the result of McMurtry rubbing up against the fence posts of his corral, but he cannot quite crawl over the slats or slide under them. These characters remain, to me, extravagant realism rather than realistic characters who suddenly transcend into magic. McMurtry has a smaller corral than Gabriel Garcia Marquez or Carlos Fuentes.

Elmer Kelton has an even smaller corral: he stays in Texas; he doesn't seem to nuzzle the edges as much as McMurtry. He has said that, unlike Louis L'Amour, who has characters who are six feet tall and sure of themselves, he depicts characters who are five feet eight inches tall and nervous. McMurtry creates characters who can elevate nervousness to mythic stature; his characters can be grandiosely nervous. It is as though McMurtry is creating his own myths, etching these characters into our literary galaxy of bright stars. They or their creator seem to have a self-conscious sense of literary destiny, or perhaps cinema destiny: the basis of Oscar-winning performances for aging stars looking for good character roles.

Texas and the myths that cling to Texas provide McMurtry with the models for these characters. Even his extravagant non-Texans have this extravagant Texas-like feel to them. This extravagance stems from folklore. McMurtry has heard the Texas stories, jokes, and metaphors. But fiction requires more restraint, and McMurtry is trying to figure out just how much restraint he needs to have. To McMurtry's credit, the old corral is leaning from his constant tampering with its posts. But ironically, the extravagance of the myth restrains him from ever kicking that fence post down.

The epic proportions of *Lonesome Dove* accommodated this extravagance. The thin narrative line of getting a herd to Montana kept McMurtry mostly on track (with a few detours) so that the extravagance seemed to match the subject matter. But in *Billy* the characters seem extravagant for their own sake, for the sake of escaping yet staying within the corral. To American readers McMurtry is like Dickens. He can create villains and superreal characters that welcome parody or play against myth; but though they serve to show social or literary indignation, their very colorfulness makes them complete in themselves, loose from mythic or social relevance, so readers divorce these characters from substance. We delight in Dickens's or McMurtry's characters but don't ask what they mean.

Since Billy is already a myth, McMurtry has to downplay the character because of the mythic baggage, so I delighted in Billy's normalcy, in fact his subnormalcy. But when he goes about creating his own characters, McMurtry destroys his realistic tone by endowing these characters with godlike prowesses.

I have yet to elaborate on what intent I sniff in the dust that McMurtry raises. In *Lonesome Dove* McMurtry took on the cowboy myth; but with *Billy* he takes on a more specific legend. And perhaps, more than with *Lonesome Dove,* the specificity of this legend and its familiarity and popularity, particularly in films, create an even more formidable problem for McMurtry. To deal with this problem he obscures historical facts, changes Billy Bonny's name to Billy Bone to buy poetic license yet keep us informed about whom he is really writing about, and, most important, creates his middle-aged narrator, Ben Sippy.

With Ben Sippy, McMurtry has a foreign point of view to register the drama. Ben looks at occurrences with a sense of strangeness that a Philadelphia gentleman would have, yet with all the mundanity and banality of a participant. He is at his best in his discussion of the massacre at Skunkwater Flats:

> *They've all made a study of it, you see, whereas I was just there. The very fact that I* was *there — it's about the only fact they can't dispute — just makes them edgy; in fact, it makes them jealous and produces much resentment. They'd all like me better if I were dead, like the other mighty men who fell that day. (p. 220)*
>
> *I try to tell them it was just a long hot boring day, with a certain amount of fear mixed in — after all, I was squeezed into a sweltering cabin with a horse and a dead man and a bunch of moody gunfighters who made very little effort at conversation. (p. 220)*
>
> *That's what occurred, but its not good enough for History. The Battle of Skunkwater Flats has been studied as if it were Waterloo, or at least the Custer fight. They've measured it all with their calipers and are not happy to have an actual participant around to question the measurements. (p. 221)*
>
> *They're part of legend now, the sweethearts who died at Skunkwater Flats: they died and were raised to glory; I lived and became deflated and old. It's a melancholy thing because, hard though they were, I liked those gunmen who died in that windy gully. They only warred on one another, as near as I can see, and they brought some spirit to the ragged business of living, a spirit I confess I miss. (p. 223)*

McMurtry, through imagination and craft, must closely approximate the excitement of what really happened. A good history of Billy, one like Evan S. Connell's *Son of Morning Star,* would be the most intriguing account of Billy because it would achieve a more factual rendering of his less than romantic reality. But McMurtry is also interested in myth, and thus his fictive narrator also provides insights into myth.

Ben Sippy writes dime novels, so he helps create myths by distorting truth. In fact, Cecily and a nun read his books that distort the reality they are stuck in and find excitement and truth in them. So Ben—when he discusses his life, observes his cowboy heroes, or tells us about his novels—constantly juxtaposes reality and myth and the tension between the two. Then when we realize that Ben is myth or perhaps a potential myth because he is in a McMurtry book, we get confused about which is more real: myth or reality. This is McMurtry's point.

But McMurtry also uses Ben Sippy to comment about the effect of the tension between myth and reality on the mythmaker. Like McMurtry, Ben Sippy nudges the corral. In fact, he may become a devise for self-criticism, a means for McMurtry to criticize his own work. At the end of the novel, in nineteenth-century fashion, is the writer's signature, but the signature is McMurtry's, not Sippy's. So McMurtry again leans heavily against the fence post of his realistic corral. *Anything for Billy* is not just Sippy's reminiscences but McMurtry's novel. It is both realistic and reality shattering.

Ben, now with Larry's signature, gives something of a eulogy to McMurtry's and all writers' careers and truths. McMurtry says in lectures that novel writing is a middle-aged activity, that the writer reaches literary maturity in middle age but exhausts it before he reaches old age. Ben Sippy discovers the "real" West and "human depth" in middle age during his trip to New Mexico but bumps into the limits, his own corral posts, in old age.

Sippy has seen the real Billy and Billy's real death and tried to write a real novel, which we should expect, due to Ben's style, is overwrought and overly dramatized. He, after all, coins the nickname "Billy the Kid." Ben states that, despite his literary pretensions, he fails at literature and leaves only a few notable dime novels, although he does find something of a resurrection with his nearly accidental collaboration with the movies. Like Ben Sippy and his version of the "White Star of the West" (Billy the Kid), McMurtry created grandiose characters out of legends or mixtures of legends and imagination that in turn made McMurtry even more popular and more rich through the movies they inspired. McMurtry's extravagant characters became great roles for stars wishing to act or character actors looking for better billing: Paul Newman, Patricia Neal, Ben Johnson, and Shirley MacLaine. McMurtry cons both Ben and the movies. He shows us Ben's insight into "human depth" but failure to reproduce it in literature or to recapture the heart of his recalcitrant wife, Dora. And if Ben is the butt of these jokes and is a stand-in for McMurtry, perhaps then McMurtry critiques his own sense of failure in dealing with a Texas or western myth. McMurtry is perhaps his and his subject matter's best critic.

Finally, Billy is like McMurtry's Texas background. Preprogrammed to be mythic by McMurtry's technique and his own legend, Billy just can't quite live up to anything. Everyone in the novel will do anything for him, but he is limited by his own ordinariness. For this reason, for his pathetic nature, I like him more than many of McMurtry's fully blown characters who beg to be myths. Ben Sippy loves Billy yet is disgusted by him, wants to dispel the myths about him but helps nurture them, desires to look at "human depth" within Billy (his ordinariness) but winds up corralled by the myth and the mythmakers. As Ben Sippy says, "I suppose they'll argue it forever—or until all the black dirt of life finally washes off Billy and leaves him a pure, clean legend" (315).

So in *Anything for Billy* McMurtry, perhaps consciously, complains about being trapped as a Texan, as a Texas writer, or as a myth. Unlike Benton and Zinberg et al. from *The Yellow Rose,* he knows what he is up against. He bitches about his Texas literacy roots in his two most uprooting essays, "Southwestern Literature" and "Ever a Bridegroom: Reflections on the Failure of Texas Literature." Yet he loves the past, as is evidenced in *Lonesome Dove, Anything for Billy, Horseman Pass By,* and all the rest. Thus a Texan is corralled because of the way that the rest of the country sees him. He is corralled because of the way other Texans see him. He perhaps even corrals himself. Yet he likes the old, scarred boards. So any narrative about Texas—whatever Texas it deals with, whether myth, reality, nostalgia, Old South, or Old West—must confront the myths and overcome them. What is real, what is myth, and what people think is myth and real get many storytellers lost.

In the old dust jacket Larry sits on a Texas corral post and looks incapable of literary deeds. Like the Kid, he looks to be just an ordinary guy stuck with his peculiar obsession. McMurtry sits on the corral, not content to jump into the middle of it or jump off of it. But he has some virtue and some insight from his vantage point. For years McMurtry has been nuzzling the corral, climbing up onto its posts and standing in it, but always within its confines. Maybe some new Texan will kick the damn thing down without losing sight of it.

The Hispanic *Seduction* of the Southwest

Except for a three-year period in Oklahoma and a three-month stint in Los Angeles, I have spent my life in Texas, first in San Antonio and Central Texas, then in dry, shadeless West Texas, specifically in Odessa, and now in muggy, southeastern Texas in Beaumont. In Beaumont, which is more of the Old South and less of Texas, I don't see many Hispanics, and the Hispanicism that I do see seems adapted more to Americanism. I miss Hispanicism. No Texan can resist talking about Texas, and no blue-eyed Anglo Texan, such as myself, could dare discuss Texas without discussing Mexicans.

Traditionally, most Anglo-Texan discussion of Mexicans becomes the cursing of "Mexcans" or "Meskins." In the nineteenth century Anglos did far worse than simply cuss Mexicans. While researching a history paper about L. H. McNelly's actions along the Nueces Strip in 1875, I found dispatches in the *Galveston News* about activities in the area—such things as "Sheriff Brown found Mexican hung in tree. Case closed" and "Sheriff's posse found Lipan Apaches and Mexicans with horses. Indians and Mexicans killed. Horses retrieved." The curtness of the telegraphed dispatches and the assumptions that they showed are chilling.

Mixed with Anglo racism and violence in both the nineteenth and twentieth centuries and lurking beneath their derogatory discussions and labels is a profound Anglo fascination with Mexicans. The old political *patróns* of twentieth-century southern Texas cussed "Meskins": the general opinion was that they didn't think like a white man, you couldn't trust 'em, and they always had a cousin who was sick. But the same old men had a begrudging respect that eventually gave way to envy. My friend in Balmorhea, Johnny Kingston, a descendant of a long line of West Texas ranchers, is bilingual, spends a lot of his time in Mexico, and sometimes wishes, like I do, that he were Hispanic.

The academic talk about the Hispanic reconquest of the American Southwest crossed the border to this country's colleges and academic journals and then floated down from ivory towers to the barrooms and pulpits of Odessa. The idea comes as no surprise to West Texans. It scares them. "They ought to learn to speak English if they want to live in this country," I've heard. "I'm gonna put a taco on my car and drive north until somebody asks me what that thing is on my car," say xenophobic Anglos.

But most of the people who cuss Mexicans speak highly of the beauty and charm of San Antonio, my hometown, or of northern New Mexico. Meantime, San Antonio and Santa Fe are booming because Yankees come south to see a Mexican city without going to Mexico. They seek a sanitized Anglicized Mexico. The Anglicized Mexicos in this country are alluring. The tourists come and the barroom domino players complain not because of a cultural conquest but because of a cultural seduction. And a seduction, which always arouses something personal in the victim, is far scarier and is a far more total defeat than a conquest.

While growing up on the south side of San Antonio, I heard Anglos cuss "Meskins" using Spanish cuss words. Like most San Antonio kids, I longed for the TV images of what America was supposed to look like: snow in winter, big trees that turned colors in the fall, and basements or cellars. At that time, the late fifties and sixties, San Antonio was under the control of its own Anglo *patróns,* the old moneyed people who had traditionally controlled city politics. These people wanted San Antonio to fit the image of a clean All-American City. But the matriarchs and dowagers of San Antonio realized that the Hispanic nature of the city kept it from fitting such an image. They tended to apologize for the city's Hispanicism; they were patronizing toward Hispanics. As a result, a lot of San Antonians felt that San Antonio was never really as good as other big American cities. We were backward, just a hick town that got big. Even worse, I and other Anglos were stuck on the south side, the poorer, mostly blue-collar part of town; we couldn't even make it to the mostly Anglo, suburban north side. The Spanish language and the Mexican rhythms around me seemed mundane while the image of midwestern America on TV seemed exotic. Even some of my Mexican-American friends cursed San Antonio, and thus indirectly, Mexicans.

Meanwhile, with all the self-loathing, Mexican cursing, teenage angst, and craving for American blandness, I was gorging on enchiladas and tacos. My mother raved about my grandmother's good ol' "German enchiladas." As a child I was accustomed to naps after lunch. During the summers I went bare-footed and bare-chested, the dirty asphalt streets and cement sidewalks staining my soles to a dark gray every day. I'd sit on the curbs of icehouses or service stations, eat a *raspa,* and listen to the discussions of my father and other men. In what *Places Rated* calls the hottest place to live in the country, neither my house nor my public schools had air-conditioning. We simply assumed that humid heat was inevitable. We learned to enjoy coolness where we could find it: in the nightly gulf breezes, against the sides of Coke or ice machines, in the shade, under freeway overpasses. Every Christmas we'd watch snowy TV specials; then we would celebrate Christmas with my German mother's relatives on Christmas Eve. Luminarias lined many of the south-side blocks. We opened gifts and ate tamales while the grown-ups and older kids drank beer. We spoke English, but the first curse words and kiddie words for excrement and nasty anatomy that we learned were Spanish.

We were more Hispanic than we thought, more than most Anglos. But we also absorbed the Anglo and Texan self- and cultural assurance that accounts for both its racism and its fascination with more mystical cultures. We wanted desperately to be more WASPish. I got better. I gave up my WASPish wishes in high school and college. I gave up a lot of Anglo Calvinism for the more seductive qualities of Hispanic passion. One of the deep regrets of my life is that, even with its musical hum all around me, I never learned to speak Spanish.

San Antonio has changed for the better. The year 1973 marks a gigantic shift, if not in the history of Texas, in the history of San Antonio because Texas Protestants lost out to liquor by the drink. San Antonio could now serve mixed drinks and could attract large conventions. Yankees would come to San Antonio to experience the Hispanic culture. What the old patróns had taught me to suspect about San Antonio was now marketable. And with new voting districts and changed politics and the Anglo realization that Hispanics represented a lot of purchasing power, more Hispanics entered city and state politics; San Antonio became truer to itself rather than what Anglo leaders wished it to be.

To Anglos, inevitably raised with New England Calvinism in their background and taught about the sanctity of business and social responsibility, the Hispanic culture offers a respite. The Anglo psychopath, sick of the pressures of his society, may find an outlet for his psychopathy in the more emotion-laden Hispanic culture. The Mexicans whom many Anglos curse just don't give much of a damn about a world other than their own. So many of them have a fatalistic but ironic and humorous acceptance of their world and the world around them. They survive. How long could *Norte Americanos* remain calm citizens with the same kind of inflation rate that plagues Mexico?

My colleague and drinking buddy Truett Hilliard often tells me about his trip down the Baja peninsula. On one span of pristine beach were mounds of rusting beer cans. Truett, being a conservationist of sorts, asked one local, as best as he could, about the trash on the beach. The man replied, "What trash?" Truett pointed to the mounds of beer cans. The man said, "It's not trash. It's cans."

Near the eastern edge of Big Bend, just before the river winds into Boquillas Canyon, is the tiny hamlet of Boquillas. Locals will row tourists across the Rio Grande, then give them a donkey ride up a steep grade to the tiny, dusty town. The one outdoor restaurant serves a good taco and lukewarm Tecates. The patio dining area has a grand view of the outhouse behind it. The owner of the restaurant does not figure that his outhouse spoils his view.

Across the street is a bar. On the walls are *Playboy* centerfolds, and behind the bar is a list of names of locals who owe money. Underneath the names is a long note that translates to something like "if you are caught in here without your money, your ass is mine." For the sake of the tourists, the bar has a men's and a ladies' room. Both doors lead outside. Customers needing toilet facilities can, if they wish, go through the doors and pee down a cliff. The cliff overlooks a tar-paper shack and the owner's dogs and goats. Lining the cliff is a layer of cans rusting from the piss and baking in the sun. The owner of the tar-paper shack sees no trash, only beer cans and people pissing.

Besides rusting cans that the locals cannot see as trash, many poor border communities abound in sleeping dogs. In Puerto Peñasco, a pleasant fishing village on the Gulf of California (as Norte Americanos say rather than the Sea of Cortés), I noticed that the dogs had a tough time finding shadows to sleep in. Puerto Peñasco is situated between the desert and the ocean. At noon the clean, dry air with just a bit of salt allows the sun to beat down without any hindrance. So the dogs, ribs sticking out, find shadows where they can go to sleep. I have seen five or six dogs, sprawled out together, in just a sliver of a shadow. Sometimes these shadows extend into the mostly dirt roads. If so, the dogs sleep in the roads. None of the native drivers seem to notice the dogs, but they grant them their dignity and their afternoon siesta by driving quietly around them. I have seen such sleeping dogs and courteous natives in Santa Fe and the small mountain towns around it and in some of the barrios in San Antonio.

In northern New Mexico on a back road from Albuquerque to Santa Fe, now nicknamed "The Turquoise Trail," are two small towns, Madrid and Cerillos, that illustrate some differences between Anglos and Hispanics. Madrid is an old mining town, a former ghost town, brought back to life by ex-hippies, drifters, and New Age types. The newcomers have restored the old saloon, which now advertises entertainment and melodrama on summer weekends, and opened a general store (specializing in health food), a Swiss bakery, and several specialty shops and restaurants. Tourists stop to take pictures of a locomotive, get a drink, or buy a meal. Farther down the road, in fact just off it, is Cerillos. Cerillos, the one-time home of Marc Simmons, never really closed down, though it still looks broken and closed. This town's population goes back to the Spaniards who first settled the area. It has adobe huts, sleeping dogs, cars on cinder blocks (the mark of poor folks across America), chickens, and signs dating back to the 1930s. Also during my visit the town had *new* signs with 1880s dates on them. The cast and crew of *Young Guns* had just finished shooting. The residents had let the movie people put up their own signs, even change the name of the one store; then, maybe because they liked the signs, the residents just left them up. Madrid was clean, proper, and pretty. Cerillos was dirty and smelly, but it seemed more honest; what quaintness it had wasn't studied. I'd be welcomed in Madrid if I moved in. But I'd be a suspicious outsider in Cerillos—if the locals let me move in at all.

Farther north, toward Taos, Indians display some of the same indifference toward the Anglo world. While I was in a bar in Taos, a man from the

Taos Pueblo asked me where I was from. He could spot a greenhorn. After I told him what I was doing in Taos, going to school of all silly things, he told me that he could rip out my throat with his bare hands—Tae Kwon Do or some such—or pray to his ancestors that I return safely home.

I affected his affected indifference and ease. I said that I hoped he would pray for me. I bought him a drink, and he bought me a drink. He told me that he was an artist and invited me to the Pueblo to look at his paintings. For a moment I played the part of the crude tourist and asked if he made money at his art. "Sure," he said. "I made $5,000 in 1979 (this was 1984), and I bought a truck," he hesitated, then added, "but I wrecked it." He shrugged. When we talked about money, profession, or jobs, we weren't talking the same language.

Just outside of Taos, on the high road between Santa Fe and Taos, was a small grocery and saloon, Virgil's. I would go inside for a beer, and I met Virgil himself, a very old man. On one stop I asked him about the date etched into the stone building, 1931. That was the date that Virgil started the bar. I thought for a moment and asked Virgil if this wasn't during Prohibition. He waved his hand and dismissed that whole silly gringo idea.

Many small-town Mexicans, Indians, even the people with old roots stretching back to the Spaniards make no distinctions between natural and unnatural. They adapt to what is. Money and the present are to be enjoyed but are always merely temporary. Compared to fast-paced middle-class, ambitious Anglos, compared even to poor, country Anglos, they have a much deeper sense of timelessness. The beer cans will eventually become sand. Money is really not important except for certain pleasures, like getting drunk. Anglos find themselves less able to adjust to pronounced change and are probably less able to let the inevitable alone.

Besides a sense of timelessness and adaptability, Hispanics have a seductive religion. Catholicism has a rank yet rich past. Its dogma about women, birth control, and papal infallibility distance it from a twentieth-century world, and yet it can incorporate the peasant as well as the intellectual through symbols and mystery. Good old-fashioned American Protestantism—whether mainline National Council of Churches or the fundamentalists—doesn't have the history or apparently the ability to see or read beauty into the Bible. Americans want the Bible to be either intellectual or literal. Latin Catholics can accept beauty as enough.

With a hierarchy, however absurd it may be, Catholicism offers advancement along that hierarchy while the more democratic Protestantism offers individual interpretation. A Catholic has a choice of where to stop or of how far to advance or of how far to grow. The American Protestant has no hurdles, so he flounders about looking for some, grows desperate, or buys into the restrictive Victorian and Puritan dictums of fundamentalists. Even the liberal churches seem merely to replace God with science or humanism and become staid because they are built upon the solid rock of rejection. In short, ironically, the more elitist Catholic Church, even with the residual guilt that it leaves in ex-Catholics, offers more of a chance for growth than does a serious Protestantism. If one has to have a firm belief, if one has to have a religion in place of philosophy or in addition to it, he is probably better off as an individual aware of himself and his own pain in the Catholic Church than in most Protestant churches. In fact, as I've often heard Truett Hilliard quoting George Santayana, if Martin Luther had not come around and loused things up by taking the Church seriously, Catholicism might have become a beautiful, complex, and elaborate set of symbols. As Santayana said, "I don't believe in Christ, but I believe that Mary was his mother." As best I can figure, Santayana doesn't believe the dictates of the Church but loves its beauty. Without a reformation and thus with a Catholic Church devoted to beauty, Emerson might have stayed a Catholic priest instead of giving up on being a Unitarian minister.

A New World Hispanic–flavored Catholicism interests me more than old World Papal Catholicism—from liberation theology to the candles with the pictures of the saints that are sold in Safeways. Even though I am a disbeliever, the Catholic artifacts seem more real. I went to a Lutheran church, primarily as a social activity, and looked at the abstract gold crucifixes and the ornaments. I even set foot in Methodist and Baptist churches and looked around in vain for any type of ornamentation. In contrast, as a child first going to the missions around San Antonio, I was scared of the crucifixes and the tapestries in the old missions' chapels. These Jesuses spurted blood everywhere. These were not smiling, pale Max Von Sydow Jesuses, but dark Jesuses with matted black hair, faces twisted in pain, and veins bulging out of arms and foreheads. These Jesuses were gods with blood, capable both of divinity and dreaming about the sexuality of Mary Magdalene. As I became older, they became less scary and far more interesting than the Protestant crucifixes.

And of course, in New World Hispanic Catholicism, Indian beliefs mix with Catholicism to produce even prettier, shinier, and wilder stories. Too bad that our Puritan forefathers' Anglo snobbery kept them off the Indian princesses so that Anglo Americans might have some neat mongrel cultural mixtures. The best example of the mixture in Texas is the mystique and belief surrounding *curanderos* and *curanderas.*

A former student of mine, Ana Camacho, gathered information about curanderos for me. She went to places where an Anglo wouldn't be trusted, and she got people to talk who wouldn't talk to me. She waited in lines formed by Mexican Texans from all over the Permian Basin to talk to one famous and popular Odessa curandero, and she conned information out of her parents and grandparents.

Ana claims that West Texas curanderos all owe a debt to the stories that surround a late-nineteenth-century curandero, Don Pedrito Jaramillo. In most Texas grocery stores there are candles stuck in glasses with Jaramillo's name written on the side. Don Pedrito is buried in Falfurias and spent his life in southern Texas, but I have heard reference to him or someone like him living in Mexico and West Texas. He is sort of an all-purpose saint who moves around a lot.

In Ana's West Texas version, Jaramillo had some incurable illness and in desperation lay down on the newly laid railroad tracks. He placed a white handkerchief over his face so that he wouldn't see the train coming, and he promised God that he would dedicate his life to curing and helping others if God would cure him. He felt the power of a healing presence and got up. Soon he began curing others with his white handkerchief. Today pictures of Don Pedrito Jaramillo holding his white handkerchief are tacked onto the walls of present-day curanderos' places of business, and some even use him in their cures or in their *oraciones* (prayers). Ana told me that in the early twentieth century the village of Balmorhea lost a large portion of its mostly Hispanic population because, supposedly, a bad curandera had placed a *malpuesto,* an evil spell, on the town for some disservice done to her.

If I were to choose a superstition, I'd far prefer to spend money for Don Pedrito Jaramillo's oraciones than for towels with Oral Roberts's handprints or Bob Tilton's footprints. Perhaps if a charismatic, camera-wise curandera could get her own TV show, she'd compete favorably with the Protestant televangelists. Perhaps, though, the strangeness of the culture would scare off an Anglo audience. The Anglo Protestant would have to abandon too many of his previous tastes. The curandero perhaps demands too much release of twentieth-century technological comfort and perhaps offers too much chance for doubt, too much self-introspection. On the other hand, as the Anglo suspected all along, belief in curanderos can lead, off-handedly, to the bizarre and tragic satanic, voodoo slayings in Matamoros. The Mexican press and police paraded the prisoners around and didn't cover up the story. They catered to the ghoulish and bloody in the Mexican public's taste. The American public, when confronted with the ghoulish in a more real form than in *National Enquirer* stories, got scared. Americans were afraid of some sort of hypnotic effect. If a person gives into his superstition, he can lose his hold on materialism and realism and get lost in the bizarre.

So the nonchalant attitude, passion, and acceptance of the Hispanic culture seem to draw reluctant Anglos toward Hispanicism even while they curse it. Besides, the Hispanic culture is pretty and the food tastes so good. Perhaps Mexicans are a little closer to what Anglo Texans work their way toward. A seduction and not a reconquest is at work. Yet the Anglo brings his culture and commercializes and sanitizes what drew him to the Hispanic culture.

Complicating the matter of maintaining a distinctly non-Anglo American culture are the traditional American desires for homogeneity, efficiency, democracy, and social opportunity. Archaeologists and anthropologists want to preserve culture, but American democrats and social reformers of any ethnicity would not want the poverty, the machismo, the superstition, and the alien values in certain cultures. In our present social climate, Americans want to preserve culture yet make the outsider into an American, and while doing so provide social opportunities. Since no government can provide real equality, we provide equal opportunity, which equates to providing equal opportunity to accept certain essentially Anglo American values. The resulting prize is usually a cash settlement. Americans find that we cannot have distinct cultures along with a technological society and functional democracy.

And despite a lot of the talk about Hispanic pride and heritage, Hispanics in America seem to be assimilating. Despite the drop-out rate and the poverty, Hispanic Americans are cutting out a literary and cultural niche in the main currents in this country. Assimilation, for good or bad, is not far away. Unlike blacks, who have almost created a repressed, alternative American culture, the Hispanics (and the Asians) seem to be the next wave of immigrants to assimilate, but in changing, Hispanics, perhaps more so than previous groups, will change Anglo America.

The Hispanics' assimilation creates strange and exciting mixtures where the Anglo and the Hispanic meet. These crazy-quilt communities and emblems are interesting to me because, although most of the resulting images and language will disappear into the mainstream culture, a lot will be absorbed. San Antonio produces some lovely mongrels.

In San Antonio, when I visit, I jog through my parents' south-side neighborhood. I particularly like one long route that takes me through several social strata. One or two main streets from my parents' neighborhood of aging Anglos is a neighborhood that is being revitalized by Mexicans. Highland Park was a classy neighborhood in the 1930s when people thought that the city would move south rather than north. But most of the post–World War II suburban development headed north and left this old neighborhood in disrepair. I remember Anglos moving away, farther north, and their yards becoming overgrown with weeds and the houses subdivided. Now Mexicans with middle-class money and some Anglos who want to escape a suburban life have moved into the houses, cleaned them up, painted, and formed neighborhood watch groups and civic organizations. The members of this new immigration do not have enough money to create the typical gentrification of some inner-city neighborhoods. They retain a lot of what they find. The homes are California-style bungalows, Spanish tiled stuccos, or high-roofed imitation English manor homes—in other words, either ornamental thirties or prefab fifties architecture. The new owners have painted the homes in brighter colors and have put wrought iron furniture on the porches and even some shrines in the front yards. Sometimes Spanish music wafts out of the houses; sometimes hard rock blares out.

As I get closer to old Breckenridge High School (named for an old Confederate), which was renamed Wheatley High School when mostly black Wheatley was shut down but is now once again Breckenridge High because of Hispanic pride in the name, the colors of the faces get mixed up. I see yuppie puppies, from the genuinely gentrified King Williams area, playing tennis on Breckenridge's/Wheatley's/Breckenridge's tennis courts. My mother went to Breckenridge when it was mostly Anglo. And during my high school days, the old, impressive, three-story high school was a mixture of Hispanic and Black. Now the restored mansions from a neighborhood even older than Highland Park stand right next to the completely rebuilt, modern high school. These new King Williams residents, who stretched the boundaries of the "prestigious" area by buying out the residents of the old, crumbling, subdivided mansions, have to have a lot of money for the restoration and upkeep that the King Williams area demands.

On Flores, Presa, and St. Mary's streets people are still poor. Babies in diapers waddle around in front yards and squat in mud puddles. Some cars on cinder blocks sit in front yards or along curbs. The restaurants sell *barbacoa* on Sunday. And mixed in, left over from older, more prosperous times, are some religious gift stores, an office equipment company, and a German restaurant. The most remarkable image of gentrification, middle-class realignment, and changing faces was just on the border of the King Williams area. The Beauregard Bar was a trendy bar that ex-hippies, Hispanics, punks, and college students frequented. Across the street from it was—by south-side San Antonio standards—a rather posh Mexican restaurant. And on the other side of the Beauregard was the *Septembre Deiz y Seiz* laundry. This was a coin-operated laundry with mostly poor customers, but the wall facing the Beauregard was covered with a mural celebrating Mexican independence, complete with the Mexican eagle and snake and Father Hidalgo. On my last visit I saw that the Beauregard Bar was closed and the mural was painted over.

San Antonio also originated a sort of Mexican McDonald's. The Taco Cabaña's, Sombrerosa's, Tacasita's, and their imitators are booming. Crowds gather on the patios of the twenty-four-hour fast food joints serving a large selection of Mexican food, beer, and decent machine-made Margaritas; and cars line up to pick up orders to go. The food is good enough and cheap, the service is fast, and the atmosphere, though rushed, doesn't make you feel ashamed to be an adult in a place like this. And though sometimes surrounded by traffic and car fumes, a customer can sit outside. Also a few old icehouses are holding their own against the convenience stores. Before widespread air-conditioning, the icehouses offered a cool wall, cold beer, and maybe ice cream for the kids. Whole families would gather in front of them just after sundown, sip something cold, and sit outside in the summer breeze. The clean, shiny, sterile insides of the convenience stores and the long rows of fast food shops in most towns make me miss the San Antonio neighborhood icehouses and the booming Taco Casas.

Odessa is newer; like most of West Texas, it was developed after air-conditioning. Though the climate is hot and dry (thus fairly comfortable compared to humid San Antonio), Odessans want to drive from their air-conditioned homes in their air-conditioned cars to pick up some groceries at an air-conditioned and efficient fast food shop. Then again, because West Texas lacks shade, West Texans never sit outside. San Antonians no longer have to sit in heat, but the traditions of cooling off before refrigerated air have given Central and South Texans a more sensitive tuning to their environment. They appreciate shade. The residual enjoyment and the tradition push San Antonians outside.

In Odessa only Ronnie Lewis, with his restaurant y cantina, Dos Amigos, realizes the ambience of Hispanic and Anglo cultural mixing and the pleasure of sitting outside. Ronnie converted an old stable into a large fajita, hamburger, and beer joint. He built most of the place with its large central courtyard himself. "Dos" looks like Ronnie got his architectural design from pictures of old western shanty towns and present-day Hispanic ghettos. Dos Amigos also sponsors bull rides, bands, horseshoe throwing contests, and chili cookoffs. As one person described it, Dos Amigos is a theme park for drunks. A West Texas city needs plenty of Mexicans to teach it the pleasures of outside air.

The language of junior high and high school kids is a great cultural mixer. The sound of voices in San Antonio has changed since I was growing up. The TV commentators and radio personalities that I remember were careful to have mid-American, Dan Rather accents so that we didn't betray ourselves as residents of an unhip little Mexican city. The place names and city names—Blanco, San Marcos, Floresville—were pronounced in Texas fashion (Blanco with a mispronounced *a,* San Marc*us*, Flores[all one syllable]ville). Now public speakers sometimes correctly pronounce the Spanish names, no doubt confusing locals and tourists, and dare to speak with just a hint of a Mexican accent.

No one is ashamed to listen to *conjunto* any longer. Flaco Jimenez is a local celebrity. In fact, the accordion has even drifted over into Anglo music. Once and forever hippie Augie Meyer plays country polkas on an accordion, pulling in German and Mexican fans. For his nationwide semihit, Augie listened to Anglo mispronunciations of *que paso* to sing "Hey Baby, *Kep Pa So.* / I thought you were my *numero uno Vato.*" Augie sings with a country-western accent and parodies the way that Spanish has crept into English to become some sort of unrecognizable new lingo. Flaco and Augie even join Doug Sahm and Freddy Fender to make money selling their Texas Tornados albums. And Linda Ronstadt sold a lot of copies of her Spanish album (though the Yankees in Boston wanted their money back for her concert when they found out that she sang only Mexican tunes).

When regular Anglo-style American obscenities were not good enough, San Antonio teenagers, as I remember, could always resort to a few Spanish words. *Cabrón,* which literally means "goat," was a strong word in Spanish. In English it could take the place of "mother fucker." A young Hispanic installing a radio in my car told me that the closest "honkie" word to *cabrón* was *motherfucker,* or at least *mother fucker* was the strongest word that he could think of. Playing this game of linguistic association, he said that "honkies are always saying mother fucker this and that. You say something about a Mexican's mother, you gonna get cut." Perhaps it is obscene because it implies that someone who is called a cabrón is like Pan, a man-goat, who represents uncontrollable and perverse pantheism. With the horns associated with a goat, it might also refer to the opposite of the above, a cuckold. Today, to me, *mother fucker,* with all its overuse, which has stripped it of any real meaning, just doesn't quite do as nicely as *cabrón.* While I was at Southwest Texas State University, the students realized the inefficiency and dullness of *mother fucker* and the need to spice it up. For *good-bye,* we used the acronym A.M.F., short for "*adios* mother fucker."

I don't believe anyone knows all the nuances of the different Mexican uses of *chingar.* I've heard, or thought I've heard, *chingal, chingado* (with the *d* silent as in Tex-Mex and with it pronounced). "It is not like a thing," the young man installing my radio said, implying that the word was an adjective. "If I called you or this or that thing a *chingal,* it would make no sense. You just say it when you're mad," he said. It is an empty sort of exclamation like *pinche,* which usually means something cheap or nonworking. Some Spanish professors and West Texans tell me that *pinche* refers to a certain part of the female anatomy; in Spain, I hear it is a term for a washwoman or maid. Many Anglos use both *pinche* (as an adjective) and *chingal* or *chingado* (as both noun and adjective) as replacements for *goddamn.* Sometimes it becomes *chinga-chingal.* Cussing is so much more fun when a user can forget meaning and go with just sound. It is also more infuriating to the person being cussed at. *Chingale,* another form of *chingar,* can mean "fucking with," as in "don't fuck with it, you might break it." And my mother with a polite voice has used the term for bartering or bargaining rather than saying the derogatory "jewing down."

Chingar implies an assault or hit. In my junior high and high school days, San Antonio adolescent football players developed a particularly ingenious form of the word. In San Antonio public schools, football players took pride in the number of *chingasos* on their helmets. The greater the number of marks or slashes of paint from opponents' helmets on a football player's helmet, the meaner and tougher a football player was. A bruise, a cut, an abrasion, and particularly wounds left from a fight, like a black eye, are *chingasos.* In San Antonio, small children don't have "ouchies" but rather chingasos.

Pachuco is a term dear to Hispanics in Los Angeles and to a newer generation. But while I was growing up, it was a derogatory term, especially for an Anglo to use to address a Mexican. It still carries connotations of the Zoot Suiters responsible for the Los Angeles riots during World War II. And what a Hispanic sees when using the word—whether he takes pride in the word or sees a strutting, boasting dandy when using it—reveals his politics. For an Anglo to steal the word and use it, though, is insulting. A *pelado,* which to my ears came out sounding like *pilau,* is the newest, dirtiest, poorest illegal immigrant. For a San Antonio Mexican to call another Mexican a pelado was an insult. Supposedly, the word means "to peel" and as a noun connotes someone who is so poor that he had to poke through trash and "peels" and/or has "to peel" something in order to eat. I am told that in the interior of Mexico it means "skinned one," implying some sort of political, economic social abuse, those at the bottom of the caste system.

If about to fight Anglos, Hispanics in San Antonio no longer use *gringo.* The word has lost all meaning. Instead they have borrowed black words, *honkie* and *white patty* or *paddie* (I'm not sure what we were saying). I don't know how either word originated. And to San Antonio youths, whores are *putas* and queers are *jotos.* I've seen the last slur Anglicized and spelled with an *h* rather than the Spanish *j.* The youth of San Antonio have equal opportunity discrimination and derogatory labels that cross racial and ethnic lines.

Small children in San Antonio also play linguistic games. While I was working as a "coache" for a couple of summers for the San Antonio Recreation Dept., the small brown and black children who gathered at my recreation center always wanted a "konky." I'm not sure if the black families or the Hispanic families originated the word, but it sounds like it came from the South Texas Germans, who didn't give their kids "piggy back rides" but rather "donkey rides." Or maybe there is something about getting on top of a "honkey."

Though many of these words are derogatory and often used to insult, they are more the result of youthful exuberance and fascination with language. Most of the "fights" that I was in as a teenager were just verbal battles. He who could best wrap his tongue around the different words and insult the best would win. Friends would use words in mock fights that were really creative jesting games, derivatives of "shooting the dozens" or "hoorahing" that older black Americans refer to. You scored points by being quick and outlandish. I particularly remember Izzy (Israel) Valdez and David Hill using all these words while debating whether blacks or Hispanics were the best athletes (the white guys, "white patties," had already lost). David, the black athlete, ended up asking Izzy to name just one sport at which a "Meskin" did better than a "nigger." Izzy thought for a moment and said, "cliff diving. Fucking Acapulco cliff diving." David didn't miss a beat: "Leave it to a Meskin to want to jump off a fucking cliff." In debates like Izzy's and David's, insulting Anglo, black, or Hispanic culture was not the real goal; rather, the goal was to mix and match words from different groups to come up with one's own creative combination. Though this is not ordinary West Texas cussing or joking, it does exhibit, like the lingo of most urban areas, the start of creativity, the prepoetic mind stretching poetic muscles and yearning for poetry. And ultimately, though these games had their basis in racism, I think they turned racial slurs into such obviously absurd jokes that they deconstructed the racism that created the terms.

I can't be a Hispanic. I can't even speak Spanish. On the other hand, I don't want to be completely Anglo; I don't want completely mid-American aspirations or values nor do I want the prejudices of past Anglo Texans and some of the people in the bars. However, I can't escape my culture—either my San Antonian past or my American values. I can only be pleased yet (like Odessans) a bit wary of this Hispanic seduction because it may touch parts of me that scare me.

Anglo Texans curse the encroaching Mexican influence because they know that this culture might lure them and their children away from their own culture. Yet San Antonio, not with its national reputation or tourist attractions but with its older neighborhoods, Santa Fe, and spots in the Big Bend frontier are mixing both cultures possibly to make new Texan or American words, jokes, anecdotes, and stories for the twenty-first century.

The Community College "Philosophy" as Intellectual Pollutant

At Oklahoma State, the former A&M cow college where I was a graduate student, I "ran" with a diverse bunch of other graduate students from all over the country. During one beery discussion, one of my more intensely intellectual colleagues asked about my "aesthetic" concerning this or that. My best drinking buddy, Mike Cronin, laughed and said that Sanderson had the aesthetic of a plumber. As I was going through the excruciating job of trying to get an academic job, the director of composition tried to console me. "Sanderson, you're not brilliant are you?" he asked. I told him that I feared not. He said that he didn't think so. "The brilliant people have it easy," he said. "The rest of us got to try so much harder." So though I had mixed feelings about being in Texas at what used to be a junior college, I thought that I'd fit in better in a school that catered to blue-collar people rather than the intense graduate students whom I was used to.

At my first official meeting at Odessa Community College, I sat with other new employees and heard our president say that we at O.C., unlike those instructors at uppity universities, were here to "he'pt folks." So, for seven years, I he'pt folks and observed the institution that I was in and tried to reconcile it with my intellect and personality. I began to fear that I was one of those uppity university folks, that my aesthetic was not a plumber's. Ironically, in three months, I went from being an example of crudity and intellectual shabbiness to the representative of effete, cold, unrealistic intellectualism.

With their dedication to community rule and a Texas resistance to any statewide system, with their "philosophy" or mission, which puts vocational training far ahead of intellect, with 60 percent of the Texas college enrollment, with a strong lobby, community colleges best represent the values of Texas higher education. Most community college folks, though, seem to agree with my president and the Texas notions about education. The American Association of Community and Junior Colleges got Ernest L. Boyer and a committee to tell more about he'pin' folks. The Boyer report, *Building Communities: A Vision for a New Century* (*The Chronicle of Higher Education,* April 27, 1988) addresses many of the realities of community college administering and teaching and suggests positive changes that, to me, seem wise and practical to anyone involved with community colleges. But the report didn't appeal to my uppity, intellectual desire to analyze more carefully the loose bolts, the clanging and hissing sounds, or the gray emissions of the educational machine that I was stuck in. The Boyer commission's suggestions are primarily mechanical changes that alone cannot clean up the polluted educational and intellectual atmosphere that clings to community colleges. The committee members stress that community colleges should reaffirm their mission, but they don't scrutinize what most community colleges presently take as their mission: what promoters, administrators, and faculty call a community college "philosophy." Community colleges' devotion to teaching and their democratic nature, and thus primarily social purpose, the very core of community colleges, spew out the dense, smelly emissions that most pollute community colleges' educational and intellectual atmosphere.

Boyer's committee, like most legislatures and communities, sees the community college's role as an instructional bridge between high school and college or between the "real" world out in the community and college. This emphasis on teaching seems only right and logical and supposedly cures the poor education that students receive at research institutions and in high school. But because of its intentions, the community college, through emphasizing teaching, reduces education to the social or vocational rewards that it can offer. The Boyer commission even condones this attitude. Boyer's report states that those of us in the traditional arts and sciences should "understand that work is the means by which we validate formal education."

So at the community college, the joy or the terror of a faculty member's intellectual inquiry for the sake of inquiry is judged valuable only insofar as it can be put to use in the classroom. If we think, we ain't he'pin' nobody.

As colleges, especially as "community" colleges, we should, as the Boyer commission states, sponsor our communities' cultural and educational programs, debates, readings, showings, presentations, and seminars. Even more important, faculty sabbaticals and class reduction can revitalize a faculty member's intellect and keep him wondering and imagining and thus indirectly strengthen his teaching. But with our emphasis on teaching, anything outside of teaching, anything that can't be pedagogically justified, isn't funded or encouraged. Thus intellectual inquiry—whether researching, publishing, creating, or just reading—is under suspicion on a community college campus.

Ultimately the emphasis on teaching and the resulting mistrust of intellect hurts teaching. Given enough years, the teacher at a community college no longer sees himself as a part of an academic community but as a factory worker punching a clock. At the community college our graduate degrees are not seen as the start of an intellectual life but as licenses for operating a classroom. We are strict Newtonians, strict New Critics, strict Aristotelians, strict Freudians not because we have studied alternate theories and found them wanting but because we hold on to what we learned years back in graduate school.

To justify our jobs, we sometimes gossip about our university colleagues. They may be brilliant, we all agree, but we question whether or not they can teach. Thus, we too reduce all intellect to a vocational quality and aid the careerism and vocationalism inherent in our society and our colleges. Henry Kissinger has a monotone delivery, and Thomas Jefferson was reputed to have had a lisp and poor oratory. Neither man would be of any value at a community college because neither would be perceived as a good teacher. Faculty members, administrators, and thus students see no reason to bother with intellectual inquiry when it doesn't matter. Those faculty members who do continue to read, write, research, or sculpt (not necessarily "publish") despite the discouragements are the better teachers, for they participate in what they teach. The seminars, the Ed.Ds, the surveys about how to teach can't replace the vitality and confidence that comes from participation in the intellectual world.

While assessing academic prowess through counting publications is arbitrary and absurd, publication credits at least offer something to count. With even less tangible results than research, teaching is even harder to measure. High schools could be flooded with the ink used trying to evaluate teaching fairly, and still, teachers object and students leave with poor educations. We have no effective measures. At least at the school where I taught, we had a few perfunctory evaluation forms and classroom visits; but mostly, since academic work beyond the classroom didn't count, no one was measured or evaluated. The only real evaluation was student gossip, unintentionally encouraged by counselors, about who was easiest. With no evaluations, arbitrary or not, we had no merit. Faculty members seemed scared of losing pay within a merit system, and administrators feared lawsuits without a reliable measuring tool. With no merit and no evaluations, we were mostly interchangeable. With interchangeability, we were allowed no real expertise. With no real expertise, we were as much machinery as our students were products. As machines, community college instructors continue, year after year, to spit out what we know while we try to adapt to our students. We are encouraged to question our methods but not our substance.

In Odessa College's slick TV commercials, like good Wall Street admen, we tried to hustle potential students. We pointed to the number of doctors and lawyers that we had produced or the money saved and later to be earned by coming to our school; we ignored the drunks, madmen, atheists, and communists who attended our classes and might have really discovered something about themselves and the world. To encourage our products and to keep them happy, we had a variety of student help organizations. Many of my colleagues and some students complained that our students were pampered too much. This pampering won't help them in the real world, my colleagues would say. But this pampering was again the result of seeing little value in education outside of what it can earn in the "real" world. It attempted to help society by seeing students as products that will become a part of the socially sanctioned, "real" vocational world, or it tried to help the student find a social niche. The most unfortunate consequence of our own slick hustling, added to the already constant barrage of hustling in society, was that the students, especially the younger, traditional students, saw themselves as valuable only in regard to what they did or wanted to do for a living. One young man simply couldn't comprehend why my friend, Johnny Kingston, a fortyish rancher majoring in Spanish and English, would start school *after* he retired.

To cope with the emphasis on teaching in the community college, most administrators have advanced degrees not in academic disciplines but in community college or educational administration. University administration jobs are mainly closed to these people. Through boredom, poor pay, or a variety of other reasons, liberal arts professors tend to seek out the administrative posts at the universities. This university good ol' boy system leaves out the people with degrees in administrating but rewards the professor with academic credentials. So the people who get the degrees in education in how to teach or how to administrate have to take jobs in community colleges. These governors of the community college, unlike the people with aristocratic prejudices in universities, have ideas filtered through social benefit theories. Their Freud, Plato, or Skinner is filtered through the application to educational administration. Most likely, neither the administrators nor their instructors have read the original sources, nor have they come to the originals through history, political science, literature, or science but through purely utilitarian approaches. Thus the administrators distrust true education; they distrust ideas. They in turn see education as valuable only insofar as it garners those social rewards that fit within the community's status quo.

This predisposition toward vocationalism causes an official atmosphere that seems bored with ideas. But the administrators with this training don't create much policy at all, whether conducive to ideas or not. Because of the second part of community college philosophy, its dedication to democratic principles, administrators rarely get to apply their administrative expertise. Instead, they become public relations officials.

In Texas, where we are proud of our independence, we don't have a central community college system like uppity, elitist Yankees have. So because of our independence, we are checked by local ignorance. An elected, local board composed mainly of businessmen makes most decisions about the future and fate of a community college. Likewise, a savvy legislator, dependent upon votes from the folks back home, looks better and gets more contributions if he votes for money for the "locally" controlled community college rather than approving money for some uppity university with few, if any, local folks on the board of regents. A strong college president may or may not manipulate these board members, but for public relations and community support, no politically astute president can admit to running the board or antagonize it. So "community standards" and "community relations" become major concerns of community college administrators. These terms often become euphemisms for strict accordance to the social, political, or religious norms of the most vocal or powerful members of the community. Rather than guiding the community and establishing its standards, the community college panders to its prejudices. Administrators then exist to guarantee the school's allegiance to its community and thus become less like administrators and more like salesmen.

At my college our board and our community, according to our president, was dedicated to athletics. We gave a lot of scholarships to high school students who had the athletic ability but not the grades to make it to a four-year school. So the primarily black students were exploited for another two years so that they could run or shoot at the hoops while they failed more courses and again became ineligible for four-year schools. To provide scholarship money, which of course goes mostly to athletics, our bookstore overcharged faculty and students for books. And since jockstraps and jogging bras for our sexually unbiased athletic program cost far more than books or instructors, we had overcrowded classrooms in academic foundations and an underfurnished library.

In my college and community we had a lot of religious fervor, but our administrators could not legally introduce religion at Odessa College. They just could not make *O.C.* stand for Odessa Christian College. Instead they looked for secular campaigns that they could carry out with religious fervor. Every year a new committee was formed that had the zeal of an inquisition but no real power. Usually these committees had abstract names and abstract functions. We had a Staff Development Committee that spent a semester thinking of a purpose; an Excellence Committee that spent a year defining excellence; a Retention Committee that basically figured out that many of our students were ill-prepared for college. We also had a Wellness Committee that endorsed a sort of holistic wellness. It told us that we needed to be spiritually, emotionally, and intellectually well in addition to being physically fit. One of my colleagues was disappointed that our puritan committee members left out sexual wellness. In our year of wellness, we waged a campaign against smokers that led faculty and students to gather in designated smoking areas looking like the thugs and ne'er-do-wells who congregated in such areas in high schools. I fear that, in coming years, community colleges such as Odessa College will band with M.A.D.D. mothers for a purge against drinking and chase all the patrons out of the few remaining honky tonks in Odessa.

No less a reaper of the benefits of modern-day American education than

Coca-Cola provided Odessa College with a symbol of its dedication to the secular trinity of athletics, wellness, and feel-good community college philosophy. In front of the college's multimillion-dollar athletic complex is a large sign with "Coca-Cola" written across the top. Besides the time, temperature, and upcoming athletic contests, this sign, like a neon bumper sticker, flashes out trite social bromides: "Embrace fortune when she smiles, she may not return"; "God gave me problems, but he also gave me shoulders"; "Politeness is the main ingredient of culture"; "Your day goes as the way the corners of your mouth turn"; and, my favorite, "A discussion is an exchange of ideas, an argument is an exchange of ignorance" (so much for Aristotle and two thousand years of rhetoric). I am afraid that, to people who buy the community college philosophy, these secular, trite bromides pass for education. These sayings and the sign are sort of like educational hygiene, the moral equivalent of flossing. Our sign once blurted out to our women basketball players that, though "you" lost at regionals, "*your* still first in our hearts."

These prejudices and consequences would just be silly if they didn't hurt the very people whom community colleges are designed to help. Because of its allegiance to democratic principles, because of its low tuition, because of its locale, and because of its open admission policy, the community college is logically the place to offer an education (rather than merely to "help") the minority, the disadvantaged, and the older student. But community standards and the role of the community college often keep a meaningful education from these students, especially the minority student. I'd like to think of athletic scholarship money going to needy and capable local minority students.

The community college tries to be all things to all people: a junior college, offering lower-division college courses; a vocational/technical training center; a source for helpful continuing education courses in a variety of areas. As a result, community colleges rarely know just what their mission is or what they are dedicated to other than undefinable community standards. So administrators heed the most vocal groups and the type of people elected to boards: civic, social, church, and business leaders. And these people who determine community standards most want trainable employees. Thus vocation is again emphasized over education.

Giving the community what it wants, we extol this vocational or social message in TV commercials and advertisements by pompously urging our students to conform to the Chamber of Commerce's values of social function and big bucks. We ask them to chuck their values and accept ours. Common values are certainly assets to a regime, as Alan Bloom (*The Closing of The American Mind*) and E. D. Hirsch (*Cultural Literacy*) point out, but why should students toss out their heartfelt values, even if destructive, for the more shallow values of prosperity? Becoming vocationally secure in a white, Anglo, male society may be profitable but may not fit in with the values of Hispanics, Blacks, feminists, or blue-collar workers. Better students, not necessarily those with the grades, recognize this fact. Education and intellectual inquiry may also be foreign to these students, but they are able to incorporate cultural, personal, and political disparity while vocational training often causes cultural, political, and personal distress and realignment. The Black, the Hispanic, the welder, or the oil field hand warms to education when he sees knowledge as a means in itself. That knowledge and the simultaneous escape from self and enrichment of self that it offers far surpass social, political, and economic values. These students might find in art and science further expression of their slightly foreign status in this country or a manner of coping with society by offering something superior to it. But preaching education for its own sake is less likely to win converts to communal values than preaching prosperity and middle-American values to potentially Anglicized students, so education is sanitized and socialized to fit the space on Odessa College's sign and the intellect of its messages.

The dedication to democratic principles filters down into the structure of the college. In the spirit of democracy, at O.C. all faculty members served on some faddish committee, from governing staff development to decorating for the graduation ceremony. We tried to make informed decisions, but most of us simply did not have the expertise to make many of those decisions. For example, an English teacher, a welder, a librarian, and a counselor might decide together whether a physicist gets travel money to go to a particular convention. That which bound us together in our decision was our mutual ignorance about the quality, importance, or merit of what we were deciding. Similarly, most decisions were based on mutual ignorance. This ineffectiveness served as a buffer for anyone with authority: there was always a committee to blame, so anyone with some authority could avoid tough decisions. Thus most administrators never needed to practice their expertise in community college administration.

Again, we distrust expertise. We dare not allow expertise because it would contradict democracy. So we have regulations that escalate to volumes because we try to make our apples and oranges the same. We try to be fully equitable to humanists, scientists, computer programmers, welders, auto mechanics, and nurses. As a result, we have our passing fads but few innovations and little creativity, even in teaching. The innovator or creator forces us to give support, usually money or time, to her and declare her special. We are too afraid of denying our democratic principles to admit that anyone might be special or more capable than another. So afraid of blame and of expertise, ever mindful of community opinion, and thus overly cautious, we rarely add to the curriculum or try innovations in teaching. To try something new, we need a state mandate or a very successful precedent.

This dedication to democracy also intertwines with the dedication to teaching under community colleges' open admission policies. Four-year schools and state legislatures, mainly, have determined that we should supply remedial instruction. This dedication to "stamp out *literacy,*" as Texas governor Bill Clements proposed, often makes faculty members forget about any attributes other than basic skills. Many instructors fall prey to the belief that our students—because of their age or their inability—just aren't capable of certain concepts. We teach to the commonest denominators. Thus we tend to make all of our courses mechanistic, basic skills courses. Because it makes dealing with our students so much easier and causes less wear and tear on our psyches, we end up teaching history or literature like we teach punctuation or computation. Our teaching and thus our presentation of our subjects become highly mechanical. We get our hearts and minds right with social and pedagogical theory and convince ourselves that we teach basic writing and basic mathematics because these skills will make students better plumbers, accountants, or welders, not because these basic skills will lead to better understanding of the self and the world. It is as though we teach these skills as justified in themselves instead of as elements leading to what we all believed was justified in itself back in graduate school: a shakily integrated, slightly incoherent understanding.

Because of our democratic spirit and thus dependence on head counts and large numbers of remedial courses, we are concerned with retention. Like good social do-gooders, we believe that everything in America is a problem rather than a difficulty. We don't like to admit something is a gnawing difficulty that we must learn to live with; rather we choose to see it as a problem which implies a solution. We don't like to admit that people fail, even though most of us do so quite often. So we ask ourselves how we can retain more minorities or more socially, economically, or politically disadvantaged students. With estimates of from 40 to 60 percent of the population functionally illiterate in Texas, how can we expect an open admissions institution, stressing education for all people, to have less than a 40 to 60 percent failure rate? Most of these people, very sadly, as Clay Reynolds points out in *The Chronicle of Higher Education,* have all the motivation and desire but not the basic computation, reading, and writing skills ("The Long Walk to Room 114: The Realities of Teaching Remedial English in College," October 15, 1986, p. 104). Thus most will not advance beyond remedial courses. But we promise them big bucks; essentially, we lie to them. For all the clamor for educational reform, our theories and causes fail to acknowledge that our entire consumer-oriented society, which gets its doses of weighty issues from watching Phil Donahue and TV movies of the week, mitigates against education. Our schools might be a contributory cause, but since they are not the sole cause, they cannot be the sole cure.

This democratic dedication to providing equal opportunities through open admission and counseling also hurts faculty performance. With the constant gnawing on faculty livers from student help organizations, the poorly trained or just plain nervous students themselves, concern for the college's image and community standards, and retention efforts, a faculty member must, ever so slightly, semester after semester, "adjust" the standards that he set for himself early in his career or find himself choking on his bile. In any case, standards do inevitably drop.

And because the democratic spirit turns to inefficiency, the faculty members turn to cynicism and then apathy. We punch the clock and go home. Anything other than pay doesn't stir our interest. Rarely do faculty members, let alone the community, come to readings, performances, recitals, seminars, or lectures. The faculty is resigned to bitch a lot but do little. Because of the scarcity of teaching jobs, because most faculty at community colleges aren't actively involved in academia, and because community college instructors in Texas are relatively well paid, we don't want to threaten a secure job. So we remain resigned to the whims and the "philosophies" of educational theory, the administration, and the community. We have a sense of real hopelessness and helplessness in effecting any kind of change. Some of us lose faith in our subject matter and ourselves and, unfortunately, find faith in faddish politics, fundamental religion, or the latest educational theory. And even more unfortunately, a few of us confess our newfound faith in class and thus blaspheme our academic integrity.

I have no solutions. I'm not sure that we have any solutions. Maybe we just need to squint harder and sniff more than the Boyer report does to see and smell this beast as it is. Since education seeks to differentiate, to remain conservative and yet challenge, we should perhaps see it, especially in our culture, as elitist. Anyone entering a class and hoping to teach something immediately sets herself up as superior to those listening. Even the physical arrangement of the room encourages expertise or superiority. Teaching assumes that someone knows something more than someone else. We must not let our fervor for equal opportunity blind us to the nature of learning. We then could realize that high failure rates, especially with the clamor for educational reform and the elitism of excellence, will be inevitable within a community college.

Despite and yet because of our roles as teachers, faculty members' first loyalty should be to our educations and our academic interests so that we exhibit what we teach and don't fall victim to our own brand of vocationalism. And perhaps, despite all the goals suggested in the Boyer commission, community colleges need to choose just what they want to do: once again become junior colleges and prepare students for entry into four-year schools, concentrate on technical and vocational training that enhances the community, or serve as remedial institutions that provide basic skills to those who lost those skills or never found them. Maybe then, with a clear goal, a community college could find a "mission."

The problems with educating the populace and with our political beliefs make a community college "philosophy" seem a social and ideological necessity. The desire for a college that emphasizes the students and thus teaching and that is accessible to an entire community has a typically democratic and American nobility. But in our noble devotion to these American desires, we might note how fueling our educational machinery with them might pollute the air that we hoped to refine.

After my first year at Odessa College, people began telling me that I didn't belong at a community college. I was branded as too much of an eggheaded, uppity, intellectual purist. Gradually I realized that, with what many people saw as my eccentricities and uppitiness, I didn't belong. But if I don't belong, then my intellectual and creative urges, the causes of my uppitiness, don't belong. I began to notice that faculty members had to abandon or suppress these urges and find some means of expressing them completely outside of the institution—perhaps in the bar.

More recently, in 1994, I learned that the administration that I fought with had resigned or been fired. Upon the advice of the vice president for finance, the college invested in derivatives and made three million dollars in as many years. With money comes prestige, so the president okayed the investment of the college's entire operating budget in derivatives, thus bankrupting the college, costing the taxpayers their money, and sending him, along with California's Orange County officials, to an interview with the U.S. Congress. He is now, I understand, a lay minister.

"They Can't Take an Education Away from You": Sweat and Professors

Now that I appear to be an educational elitist, I'll look at my "common" background that is common for many professors. While I was growing up, my father, when feeling fatherly, would stop cussing as he was trying to fix the car or mow the grass in order to advise me about school. He took great consolation in the fact that my sister and I both brought home *good* report cards, as though our grades pulled at least one burden off his shoulders. He may have had bills, car trouble, bad plumbing, an infuriating, underpaying job, but at least his kids weren't dumb. And thus, I learned that, if I claimed to be studying, I could escape mowing the lawn or fixing the car. I'd let my father groan, cuss, and sweat. He'd tell me to keep studying because "They can't take an education away from you."

I never took his advice seriously. Sometimes public school was fun. College was more fun. And getting educated was definitely a way to avoid "real" work—like fixing a car. I still don't know what a car motor looks like (until I was twenty-one, I thought the thing up under a car hood was a *goddamn;* my mother tells me that it still is). Majoring in English and history was even more fun and even less like "real" work. I didn't have to worry about what I'd do with my education because there was nothing to be done with English and history. I saw nothing noble or mystifying in a college education like I assumed my father did. But after ten years of getting college educated and fifteen more years of working within college education, with the self- and worldly knowledge that comes with some semblance of maturity, and with the charted and determined course that maturity forces on us, I began to see just what my father meant by "They can't take an education away from you." The key to understanding my father's statement was figuring out just what he meant by "education" and what it would make me and then figuring out who "they" were.

My father grew up during the Depression, served in the army during World War II, and was seduced by the American dream in the fifties. My education was to be the fruit of his hard times. His hard times were a "working man's" hard times. As he explained to me when I first became cognizant of political parties during the Nixon-Kennedy campaign, "Republicans are for the rich man; Democrats are for the poor man." A "yellow dog Democrat," my father would say that "a Republican is just a Democrat who lost the wrinkles in his belly." I now suspect that my secretive mother voted Republican to cancel his vote. My mother's secret votes and his Republican bosses infuriated my father. FDR had made a personal deal with my father and his generation, and after the Depression and WWII (still *the* war to me and my father), my father was not about to renege on his side of the bargain by voting for anyone other than a Democrat.

FDR's and later Harry Truman's part of the bargain was the G.I. Bill. My father tried a little college but "had people to feed," so he quit. He was a *C* student in a Missouri junior college. FDR and Harry Truman made college available to the likes of my father, not just because they made money available but because they got people like my father thinking that college might be a solution to their social and economic woes and might not be so foreign to them. Then Jack Kennedy and Lyndon Johnson made college available to me and my generation through national defense loans and civil rights legislation. My father's generation had preached to my generation about college, so we saw nothing sacred about it—and nothing awesome about flunking out of it.

Some critics bad-mouth what the G.I. Bill and civil rights legislation have done to education. The G.I. Bill sent a whole new breed of students into colleges, men and later women and minorities, who wanted education to lift them onto a higher social and economic rung. So because of their growing clout, we forgot the old aristocratic ideals of an education as some ennobling quality that was good because it was good in and of itself, and began to see education as vocational training. Although, through me, my father knows more about academe, he still sees the best result of my education as my job. The critics say that unfortunately the civil rights legislation removed social barriers from some stout teachers—women, minorities, or retired military men. So these teachers left teaching for better paying jobs. And as some critics claim, less able people, trained in schools of education, began to replace them. Thus in a way, FDR's bargain with my father may have unintentionally led to our present deterioration in education.

Maybe I am a part of that deterioration, or maybe I helped to change the faculty of colleges and thus the way that college students were taught and viewed. For FDR's bargain (along with my father's hard work) put me through school, gave me what "education" I have, and created a nationwide faculty which, at least in part, had the same aspirations, background, notions, and fathers as I.

Texas colleges, primarily because of the G.I. Bill and the National Defense Loan, are full of professors who are first-generation college students. Like me, many of my colleagues have figured out just what an education is by observing their working-class parents. Our parents did not buy the aristocratic or bourgeois or (as my father would say) "Republican" notion that work was good for you. Workers have no puritan work ethic. My father worked hard for the sake of his family and for the reward that FDR promised. He didn't believe that work made him a better man, and he didn't believe that he owed anything to the Republicans who ran the company. As most working people know, as my father knows, the best thing to do with work is to escape it. "Work is meant for mules, and they turn an ass to it," my ranching friend Johnny Kingston likes to say. To my father, education was a way to turn an ass to work. So it was a delight to him to see that his kids had good grades, that they took to education, and that JFK and LBJ were also making good on FDR's promise.

So unlike some of my colleagues and fellow students who had richer parents, I and my fellow colleagues and students with poorer parents saw neither laziness and lack of ambition nor nobility and character in workers and their work. We noticed crumpled bodies, sunburned faces, and physical and intellectual misery. So we figured to be true to our parents' often unarticulated urging to escape work. Work, as any oil field hand, plumber, laborer, or even mid-level manager knows, is sweat. We saw college as a way to find a job that wouldn't force us to sweat. And in college some of us found that we could actually get paid for staying in college. Now we teach in college, and as my friend and colleague Truett Hilliard, a New Mexican from the broad plains around Portales whose father worked at a variety of odd jobs, says, college teachers have "a bird nest on the ground."

Barry Phillips—an artist and a native Odessan whose father sold tires—confesses that, as infuriated as he gets at his job, he would beg for his or any college teaching job.

As an undergraduate I met all sorts of students from around Texas. Some, I began to notice, were a little different from me and my high school friends. Primarily, they were the sons and daughters of accountants, doctors, and lawyers. The classiest mothers and fathers of my high school classmates were veterinarians, real estate agents, and dentists. In graduate school in Oklahoma, I met students and professors from all over the country and the world. I met traditional students and professors, those whose educations and thinking were supported by family, culture, and upbringing. Many of these academics, who left what I then envisioned must have been ivy covered walls and Saturday afternoons playing lacrosse, complained about the dismal university, the dismal city, and the dismal countryside. Some Oklahomans, some professors, some students, and I labeled these students and professors as Yankees. Even some of the Yankees called them Yankees. We misreckoned that it was locale and not class that separated us. Some of their class even joined our class and vice versa. Thus by the time I got out of college, I sensed that the people whom I seemed to side with had changed the nature of college. They were grateful for the stay against or the escape from the "real" world where people wasted minds and maybe bodies in work.

At Odessa Community College, where I went after graduate school, the colleague who was closest to my age and closest to graduate school was Donna Smith. She is the daughter of a mid-level civil servant. Born to rather old parents, Donna watched both her mother and father die. She thus developed a certain perspective from which to view the grand elocutions about the welfare or terrible inability of the students, the rewards of teaching, or the mission of the community college. Donna was always more interested in the best way to "fuck off." We often commented about who in our school had the cushiest position that allowed him the least amount of work and visibility and thus bureaucratic or professional buffers around him to protect his fucking off and his job. And we discussed what classroom techniques allowed us the most time to fuck off.

Donna is a very good teacher. I'd recommend her. In no way was her "fucking off" hurting her classroom. Instead I believe that she, like me, learned how to recognize trivialities (or "horse shit") and pleasures in her job and in her education and how to tell the difference. With these distinctions in mind, Donna developed methods for avoiding the trivial and engaging the pleasurable. She learned to "fuck off." She had cheated sweat. FDR had rewarded her for her father's sweat.

Like most of us in English who are trained in literature and research but teach commas and fourth grade grammar, Donna had rehearsed and memorized every class exercise, lecture, or song and dance to achieve the greatest efficiency and ease. Thus while the classroom may no longer offer any intellectual stimulation, the repetition was easy compared to the repetition of most jobs, jobs like our fathers held, and allowed for plenty of time off for real "fucking off," whether it be writing a book, taking care of the kids, drinking with your buddies, or simply relaxing.

My father envies my job. Generally the working and teaching classes who congregated on Odessa College campus or in the Odessa bars had a common respect. Some bright Odessa oil field hand, who had read some Marx, scribbled on a wall "Work is the curse of the drinking classes." He was able to mix real work and real intellect. At first, in Odessa, as Truett and Barry Phillips tell it, the regulars at Marie's didn't accept them. The regulars knew that Barry and Truett didn't do shift work, yet they could come in for a beer at midafternoon. When they found out how Barry and Truett made a living, the regulars figured that their taxes paid for Truett's and Barry's time and beers. Truett and Barry never denied this assumption; in fact they boasted about it and bought T. Tyree, Paul Johnson, and Pete Proctor beers with the state's money and their own tax dollars. They tipped Marie's waitresses. They matched the regulars joke for joke and asked about roughnecking and plumbing. So by the time I arrived in Odessa, the locals at Marie's and at other bars saw us as workers who had beaten the system. And we tried to repay the regulars at Marie's for their trust. As these retirees from my father's era die, we tell their stories or stories about them.

In Odessa my friends and I liked to drink in the old, crumbling bars—the honky-tonks, the beer bars that do not have a liquor license. Before the It'll Do closed, we liked to have a few beers (we were often the only customers) and play shuffleboard with Mickey, the owner, and her slightly retarded son, Larry. Larry always beat us. We'd tell stories about the night in the Silver Spur when Earlene told us how she came to Odessa. Back in Arkansas her husband got mean with her, so she hit him with a shovel and drove to Odessa. After winning a horseshoe match, Truett once boasted to some blowhards that we ought to play shinbone horseshoes. Instead of a stake, you stick out your leg and use your shin. If you flinch when your opponent gets a ringer, you automatically lose. We often discussed the cold night that we sat in Odessa's sleaziest bar and shivered in the wind blowing through the cracks in the wall. We huddled over our beers and listened to Hap Smith as he sang his original composition, something about two drunks staying in a hotel. One drank the ink and sure was blue; they walked down a trestle, and one complained about the low banisters on the flat stairs. Then Jim Newell came in and, with a clear, clean voice that quivered just a bit, sang old Lefty Frizzell songs.

This milieu, these anecdotes seem true and rich to us. All of these experiences form, as Hilliard says, "threads in the rich tapestry of life." They are unabashedly romantic. They remind us from whence we come. They are truer than much of what we study or teach. We know that what we teach has its roots in the elemental concerns of our working fathers. We have no strong allegiance to sophistication, urbanity, or academe. Essentially, because of our backgrounds, we have no traditions other than our profession, so we make our own. We tell about these incidents, these places, and these people because the telling is as important as the occurrences. All of my close academic friends like to eat, drink, and tell stories. We tell the same stories and anecdotes again and again until they become lies, the same type of lies that make up legends, characters, or novels.

After a few beers, Truett always said that life was made up of two types of tragedies: unbearable tragedies and bearable tragedies. The unbearable tragedy is the truth, reality. It is the fact that cosmic time eventually erases everything. Even memories fade. As the good Texas playwright Preston Jones said shortly before he died, "Time is a son of a bitch." We make the unbearable tragedy into bearable tragedies through lies: philosophy, literature, history, and art. The truly intelligent people recognize creativity and intellect as lies but delight in them all the same. The jokes of West Texans, the suffering of Job, or Sir Gawain's adventures are all grand and glorious lies. With our exploits and our telling about these exploits, we create our own bearable tragedies. The working-class people whom we come from pretend to save their souls with the same elemental drinking, eating, and fucking that in turn become elaborate, almost true stories. We tell our stories over and over and often bore wives, husbands, girlfriends, preachers, and people with middle-class aspirations. People call it bullshit. My father doesn't like the fiction I write or the fiction that I read, but he seems to like my stories, my bullshit. In drinking, eating, "sexing," as a ladyfriend says, and then talking, we create our own myths. We make an unbearable reality bearable by making it aesthetic.

The "they," who, according to my father, are always trying to take something from us, don't understand the use of telling stories. For my father, "they" were his bosses or the executives who ran the company. Many times "they" were college graduates with business degrees who didn't understand my father's "real" working world. My father didn't realize that "they" had a different "real" world than his. To my father, "they" were always Republicans because, no matter how they voted, "they" had lost the wrinkles in their bellies and would disgust FDR or Harry Truman. "They" could make working conditions deplorable, could be completely indifferent to the dignity of the workingman (or woman), and could underpay a worker in order to keep him enslaved. Thus they could sap a worker of his youth, put her into debt, keep her mind numb from doing repetitive tasks, and cheat him of a future. So to my father, an education could strengthen a worker's own self-resolve and ultimately lift a worker to the same stature as "they." To my father, my education could put me into the ranks of "they," where I might take a few punches for my father and FDR.

But I used my education and my resulting squinting view of my life to make myself as separate from "they" as possible. Even my father has recognized that, with my study of liberal arts, I don't have to deal with a "real" world and with his "they." My father is happy for me.

But "they" still exist for me. In academe they are administrators. Administrators, like most bureaucrats, surrender their education to a practical view of their small pond. Most vocationally trained people confuse vocation and avocation; administrators at some time in their lives and educations must have known the difference; many must still know the difference, but the lines become hazy for them. They too are concerned with their "real." Theirs is the "real" world of finances, grants, coordinating boards, legislatures, and images. Administrators, probably from necessity, are opposed to the likes of my friends and me, probably because of our differing temperaments. Thus my bosses have a more difficult time with me and yet are more dependent upon me than my father's bosses were dependent upon him. My administrators often accuse my friends and me of being indifferent to their real managerial world. We are. The administrators' world, a world without anecdotes and stories, is far more abstract than my mythic world of illiterate but agonized students and barroom discussions.

Administrators, like my father's bosses, become upper-middle-class Platonists. They want the world, no matter where they live, to conform to some middle-class value system that governs "The Republic" in their minds. They crave a vanilla flavored world, a world without tragedy, a world where time is not a son of a bitch. They want to rob action of consequence and thus take away risk. Thus they want a tame world without beauty. So they don't like stories. They will probably win, but not without a fight.

Actually they are vital to any political system, and certainly any college is political. And if they would stick to managing and financing, what they are usually trained to do, life at colleges, for me and my friends, would be a lot less annoying. But inevitably they become public relations men, unable to resist the temptation to try to incorporate their notions of civility, sophistication, and education upon the colleges that they direct. They join the Rotary Club, the Lions, the JayCees, church groups, and Who's Who lists. They worry about the college's image and standing in the local, state, or academic community. In other words, they try to make the college pleasing to the Rotary Clubs, the Lions, the JayCees, and the First Presbyterian Church.

At Odessa College, where social do-gooding was a vital concept to education and where athletics at the community college level were taken seriously, the administration had a symbol of the college's values. This sign, which I mentioned previously, flashes out trite sayings that proper middle-class Christians would take as commendable: "A man of words and not deeds is like a garden of weeds"; "He who spares the guilty threatens the innocent"; "It is not so much how much you know about life but how you live your life that counts"; "Courtesy can be understood in any language"; "There is a lot to be said for both money and glory, only you can take glory with you when you die"; "Failure is not falling but staying down"; "It is not what you have lost but how you value what you have left"; "It takes a whole life to learn how to live." To Platonic middlemen, these tips pass for education.

Across town, the University of Texas of the Permian Basin had loftier ideals about education. The administrators at UTPB (and some faculty members) sought to turn their commuter school into a school worthy of the University of Texas label. The administrators had a vision of how the campus of a UT school should look. So once a year, maintenance workers sweat to bulldoze the mesquite, cacti, and undergrowth around UTPB's jogging trail. The scenery in West Texas has never inspired much lyric poetry, but it is endemic to West Texas. With the undergrowth centipedes, quail, and rabbits inhabited the area. Once an area is bulldozed, the wildlife flees; the trees have no small blooms; and the ever-present wind stirs up the dust to choke joggers. I have heard that the bulldozing was done to clear the area of smaller mesquites so that larger ones could grow and so that rabid skunks wouldn't hide in the undergrowth. But I believe that the bulldozing occurred because the administrators' visions of their campus did not coincide with the undergrowth. Flat is better than scraggly. So the administrators at UTPB dared to wage war against the environment of West Texas. The members of the Odessa Chamber of Commerce, TV promoters, preachers, and the administrators at Odessa College and UTPB didn't want to see a real, vital West Texas oil town, but instead they wanted to see what they have been told they should want to see. They will never see much beauty.

To those of us who look for beauty in bars and in mesquite, this tunnel vision with a mirror at the end of the tunnel is infuriating yet amusing. Barry Phillips and I grew indignant. My father is in me enough to make me want to take some macho, kick-ass punches at administrators. And like my father, I regard administrators, no matter how they vote, as Republicans. They have no wrinkles in their bellies.

Several times Barry, a big, bearded, impressive West Texan, clenched his teeth and fists while listening to our vice president. In a committee meeting with our vice president, I liked to cuss in front of him but not necessarily at him and to pull the stuffing out of the padded chair next to me. After a whole semester, the vice president cussed too (though the words sounded flat coming from his mouth); the chair next to me was also flat. Barry and I started petitions, complained to the faculty senate, and wrote letters to the newspaper. I wrote scandalous articles like this one, which no administrators would ever read. Barry wrote memos that got lost in bureaucratic black holes. We got little or nothing changed or corrected. So we took pleasure where we could find it, in the bars, and thought of mean, petty, but funny tricks to pull. We never did anything worthy of our imaginations.

Truett Hilliard and Donna Smith probably had the best approach to administrators. Truett accepted their ultimate ineffectualness and used quips to make them look absurd. During the phase in which administrators were supposed to get friendly with faculty members, our vice president came to see Truett. After the usual pleasantries, Truett returned to grading tests, and the vice president remarked candidly that he knew the faculty thought administrators didn't do anything. Truett made no response but kept grading tests. Unable to take any more silence, the vice president said, "We do things." Truett simply nodded and went back to his tests. The vice president then begin to sweat and tried to list his duties for Truett.

Back in the early seventies, Odessa College was trying to hold the line against creeping liberalism by keeping coeds out of jeans and in skirts. The dean met with various faculty members and scolded them for not enforcing the school's dress code. He explained that this dress code was a serious matter, that jeans on coeds incited rape. Truett Hilliard asked if the dean had ever tried to get a girl out of her tight jeans who didn't want out of her tight jeans. "Those studs in those jeans would tear off your fingernails," Truett said. It was a lot easier just to flip up a girl's skirt, Truett explained.

Donna too knew what she was up against and was content to laugh at what she was forced to do: like serving as the secretary for the faculty senate because she was an English teacher and a woman and then writing minutes and memos full of the passive voice constructions and euphemisms that administrators like to use so much. Donna knew that, like the sentences she was forced to write, administrative policies were hazy and indecipherable, and thus usually weren't enforceable. She was not always passive. Donna Smith married one summer, and upon the first full faculty gathering, the vice president congratulated her on her marriage and asked what her new name was. "Smith," she growled. All of us—Truett, Donna, Barry, and I—were honoring our fathers when we tried to take our swipes at "they."

My father may not know education as I now know it; he may not know just how education has affected me, and his "they" may not be my "they," but he was right: "They can't take an education away from you." Because of our educations and our fathers, my friends in college teaching and I are changing or have changed, for better or worse, college education, not only in Texas but in the entire country. Baby boomers or World War II babies, we all saw college as a way to strengthen our minds so that they wouldn't bend quite as much from the foibles inherent to our society and as a way to preserve our backs from bending over with real work. We know the cost of sweat. We know what bars to go to in order to see what a lifetime of sweat can do to a person. Because we can simultaneously see tragedy and humor in these workers and drinkers, we will continue to lie to ourselves, know that we are lying, and thus conjure up beauty. Since World War II, we have flooded the colleges to get our degrees and our educations because we learned quickly what both could offer. Now we compete, sometimes good-naturedly, sometimes a bit treacherously, for the scarce college teaching jobs. Demographics didn't make college teaching jobs scarce. The aspirations of our fathers, which changed our vision of the world, and the promise of FDR, which gave us the means, sent us to school and made teaching jobs scarce. So my friends and I are living off the reward that FDR intended to give to my father.

We are, in our way, as Twain said of steamboat captains, the most free men or women in the world. Our educations, our assumptions, and our jobs let us get as far away from our society as we can, maybe as far away as we dare. We don't live in an ivory tower because we remain familiar with the real world of work. But since it is not that we can't and thus don't but that we would rather not, we teach. And ironically, my father admires us because we have found a way to live within the system yet escape it as much as possible.

Students

CHASING GRADES AND LOOKING ASKANCE

By now my readers, like my students at Odessa College, may sense some demilitarized zone in my psyche between the patrician elitist who bad-mouths community colleges and the plebeian good ol' boy who tries to escape sweat through education. Students and some acquaintances at Odessa College often wondered how I could be pleasant in public or in the classroom yet discuss such airy, egg-headed stuff and leave brutal, bloody marks on papers. Among students I had a reputation of being like an Attila the Hun of English.

Sometimes I defended myself. I reasoned that I didn't want to cheat. I reasoned that, like me, my students saw education as an escape and thus deserved as good, and thus by necessity as tough, an education as some New England blue blood or at least as some Republican doctor's son or daughter enrolled at S.M.U. or Rice. While I was a college freshman, I placed out of certain classes or got easy instructors. I paid for these two lucky breaks much later.

However, I thought that my colleagues and I should not deny our students their dignity as citizens and as adults by insisting that they honor learning or our subject matter as we did, and I thought that we should allow them the freedom and the consequences of treating our classes as they saw fit. But neither should I have to give up my hard-earned values. So I was looking for a few good men, or at least some mediocre men who could learn about comma splices. But at an open-admissions college where G.E.D. students, nervous mothers, vets, and students with mental problems hoping to use school as therapy sat in my classes, I found that very few were prepared for boot camp.

Truett Hilliard, of course, concocted an on-the-spot theory as to why so many students fail at Odessa College and across the country. According to Truett, without ever having heard of Gandhi, American college students are using his methods of civil disobedience to defeat the American educational system. With an intellectual and emotional form of civil disobedience, students blithely fail or drop out of college and leave those schools in the ineffectual position of the post–World War II British. The students flood into and then out of college and slowly erode the content.

Students at Odessa also had their opinions as to why they fail. I invited students to voice their concerns or critique my class. One student said simply that I was too intellectual when I started her class, but I got better as the class progressed. I think that she ironically both condemned and praised my class. Another student from East Texas suggested that older Odessa students just didn't know no better. They had never seen a real university in a real college town where there was booze, broads, dope, trees, and water. He suggested motivating Odessa students by showing them something other than dry, barren Odessa and boring O.C., sometimes referred to as *O*nly *C*hoice College.

The students who did well in my classes sometimes felt as though they had proven themselves to be good men and so grew uppity and defended me. They too had theories as to why many of their cohorts left my classes. Most of the students who stayed with me and got something from my classes, no matter what their grades, were potential ne'er-do-wells, drunks, or perverts. In an evaluation of an American literature class, an older student with a lot of firsthand experience studying psychopathic behavior suggested that, like Mailer's psychopath in "The White Negro," I had worked through many of my neuroses and discarded much of what society told me that I should want and should do, so that I looked at ambiguities and difficulties in literature and life. Most of my students, though, not as free from social neuroses, wanted socially sanctioned and simple problems and answers. Most students were just too much the social robots to appreciate anything beyond rote. Obviously this student listened to my sermons and was at least temporarily converted. So, of course, I thought that he had a point.

I couldn't explain why I helped the students I did or why I had no effect on other students. I didn't worry about motivation or results; I didn't trust the measurements that we used. I assumed that any teacher, even at an elementary level, had to assume certain communicative abilities in his students, from the ability to spot colors to the ability to read. Sometimes, given my methods, content, and presentations, unprepared students needed a net to catch the pesky, obscure words flying over their heads. Sometimes though, even with unprepared students, I clicked. They became interested. They may even have majored in English. Some sought me out for advice. Some dropped out of school and never came back. But for some reason or another, we really liked each other and shared or discovered some knowledge.

Like Truett Hilliard, I saw teaching far more existentially than most educationists. Certain students, for a certain time or space, for whatever developmental or psychological reasons, respond to certain teachers. It was sort of like friendship. Who can tell who will be his friend from a simple description of character? I can make some general statements: A boring person will probably be a boring teacher; a person who has no interest in teaching probably won't click with students; a person with complete disdain for his students won't click; but an open, amused mind attracts other open minds and maybe pries other semiclosed minds open. Any teacher then should have an easily amused mind.

As for students, I find that no matter what their grades, I.Q.s, or ages, those students with a sensitivity and a sense of self that create a view that doesn't run parallel to their world are the most likely to get "educated." The students who get educated, my friends, and thus I (here are my prejudices) are like the father and son in Thomas McGuane's *Ninety-Two in the Shade.* Both father and son like to look at life askance; they like to watch the lateral movement rather than the forward movement in football games; and they try to get to the one right and true path by following and then discounting all the wrong paths. Looking askance may make your vision fuzzy, but it might be closer to some truth than seeing what you're supposed to. At least in looking askance you see in more of your own way.

The problem with most "educated" people, whether they are teaching, studying, or administrating, is that they approach school without wanting to define "self" fully by comparing it to the world that is not self. So their parents, administrators, coordinating boards, policy, school systems, or grades determine what an education is, and thus they surrender self to educational pablum. Bureaucracy can create a comfortable, warm spot for the egos of students, faculty, and administrators.

Without a sense of what their world is, with a real education eluding them, students will naturally have to make an education hurt in order to learn something. Some don't like the pain. Younger students often assume a smug indifference. What I have to say could not have any reference to their youth-intoxicated world. I don't mean to bad-mouth a youth-intoxicated world. A youth cannot just simply escape his youth; he cannot disregard his bubbling hormones and energy. Despite what some suppressed teenagers, right-to-lifers, Nancy Reagan, and the Ector County school board said, young people (even those approaching middle age) cannot "just say no." Unless they take a chance now and then in a dangerous world, these students will always see education as abstract and impersonal. So most young students, who like quick and easy lessons that they can memorize, are more interested in their youth, and rightfully so. The brighter ones can simultaneously or maybe in increments consider what they learn while playing out their own youthful exuberance. These are the lucky ones. Most flunk out.

Some students make good grades but for all the wrong reasons. These are the neurotic, sometimes religious high school students who said "No." A lot of these students hang out at the Baptist Student Union. They can memorize but not learn. Robert Flynn, who teaches at Trinity University in San Antonio, told me that he didn't like the new students at Trinity since it had changed from an expensive party school to an expensive National Merit scholar school. "They think only from their eyebrows up," Bob said of his students. Some older students resemble these grade chasers. Some older students, usually women, are looking for some new way to be successful, to feel good about themselves, to redefine themselves somehow. These students, young and old, take graduation ceremonies, even those for an associate degree, seriously.

These students are not always the selfish vocationalists that critics say they are. The students with the ability to pass but who have been told what an education is equate education (as well as art) with some sort of moral good. For them, moral good is the same as religion, psychological self-help, or social usefulness. And they believe that in a Calvinistic world that is right and just, anyone who aspires to the moral good will be financially rewarded. They are not nearly as Machiavellian as M.B.A graduate students. For most, school is therapy. So they are shocked, at least in my English classes, when their moral good does not match my notions of grammar or literature. They are not used to seeing questions. They want tangible problems with easy solutions. They have given up self to a grade or a belief.

One semester, after turning in my grades, I returned to my truck to find that I had a slashed tire. I suspected that some student had gotten even. Earlier that semester, while I was at a big party in a bar with Hilliard, a few other college friends, and the local clientele, I said hello to a former student, an older woman with several kids. Debi, slightly drunk, gasped at the sight of me. In front of my friends and hers, in a public place, she wagged a finger at me and told me how I had ruined her life. From what she said, I guessed that she had been enrolled in one of O.C.'s vocational programs and had made all *A*'s. Unfortunately, Debi had signed up for my freshman composition course without being warned about what a grade-stingy ogre I was. She had made a *B* (so much for my reputation as a grade miser). This *B* was an insult to her integrity, something she obviously didn't deserve. But because of it, she got discouraged and dropped out of college even though she needed only two more classes. It was all my fault. I remarked that I felt complimented she had allowed me to have so much power in her life, and one of my bar ladyfriends shot the finger at her (so much for witty responses).

I do not begrudge Debi her anger at me. But she really didn't have an honest anger. Everything that she chose to make important was a way to escape her own foibles and weaknesses. She did not want questions to her notions about herself and her value in her world. After she accosted me, I remembered her. She had chewed on my liver for an entire semester and, like many students, admitted that she couldn't write well and didn't understand but begged for an *A* anyway. I owed it to her based on her sense of what she needed.

The real irony was that she could write well enough; she did have a flare for the language and its structure (for which she got a *B*). If she had given up some of her predispositions about herself and the subject, she would have written better essays. She would at least have seen more to write about.

In the same class with Debi was another "older" woman in her mid-thirties who had dropped out of school in the ninth grade to get married, have kids, and subjugate her life to her husband. In order to remain inferior to her spouse, an out-of work oil-field hand, Anita had to be "dumb," and she admitted her dumbness everyday in class to anyone who would listen. But in studying language, she realized that she already instinctively knew a lot about it and about the world. Anita was crude but not dumb. So as language became a more useful and easy tool for her, the world started shifting into new and more intriguing shapes. For her last essay she read Alan Bloom's book along with E. D. Hirsch's *Cultural Literary* (finding out from Hirsch's questions that she was a lot more literate than she had thought) and several articles about college education from the *Chronicle of Higher Education,* and she wrote a remarkable essay about the possible problems with the education awaiting her daughter. But along with her insight came more arguments with her husband about school and growing absences from church. Anita didn't sign up for any classes the following semester. She consciously chose to remain "dumb." She had learned the consequences of education.

Moreover Anita could make the distinction, unlike Debi, between herself and her writing. Because language is such an integral part of our understanding, many people let their language make them. I realize that I am encouraging a debate between grammarians, structuralists, poststructuralists, linguists, and stodgy, blue-haired old grammar teachers; but even scholars, even if they believe that we are no more than our different "texts," recognize or at least debate the distinction between the language and the speaker. For sheer pedagogical ease, a teacher should make the distinction between the writer and the word because most students have never heard of such an assumption. So many students have such an instinctual and institutional attachment to their language that they see it as *their* language, as something uniquely a part of them. And with an *F, C,* or even *B,* I insult their notions about themselves. I often hear from a student that he "just doesn't make *C*s." I congratulate him on his first *C.* I couldn't insult Anita in such a manner. She questioned more. She took to heart my digressions in class about language both as a tool for the user and as the shaper of the user.

Some of my students who did become educated, whether because of my class, another, or their own efforts, have scored some points against the grade-chasers. One student who liked me recommended me to a friend who was studying nursing. The friend, used to memorizing the names of drugs and body parts, made a *D* and told my former student, "Jim Sanderson can just stick his *D* up his ass." My student made me proud of her when she replied, "You know, Jim might like that." Two female students who ended up majoring in English at the upper-division college across town ran into a rather staid woman in one of their classes who said that she would have taken my class but she had heard that a female had to be young and pretty to pass, like the two whom she was addressing. This student was old, frumpy, religious, and searching for excuses. My two former students recognized as much in her not so subtle insult. They replied that I did indeed have standards and that no female passed just for being young and pretty; a woman in my class, even if she were young and pretty, had to "put out" or she would not make her *A*. Somehow I think that these students have achieved a victory over liver-eating neurotics for themselves and for me.

For the grade-chasers, then, education or school becomes another impediment to education. Within most colleges, though, we have various means to fuel and otherwise encourage these students' neuroses. At O.C. counselors helped with this task. Our counselors gave "practical" advice about how to pass whose class and about whom to take in the first place.

One of my more nervous students, again an older lady, having trouble writing coherent paragraphs, sought help from the counselors. Someone told her that her inability was not really her fault nor really mine. The fault lay in varying expectations. I demanded professional standards in my basic freshman composition class. The student momentarily felt good because she had no desire to produce professional-quality writing. She simply needed to find someone without professional standards, but she would first set me straight. When she informed me of what she had been told and that professional standards—such as full sentences and coherent paragraphs—just are not fair criteria for freshmen, I felt sorry for her. The counselor's ill-chosen words soothed the student but robbed her actions of consequence and thus robbed her of individuality or significance.

But many of our schools believe in such soothing. Counselors and social do-gooders can always adjust a comment or a measurement to accommodate the height and weight of simple personal esteem. Most important to the school, though, this student, unlike Anita, who saw real problems, did sign up for another semester and thus paid her tuition and added her head to our count. She happily continues to pass, probably without learning.

During my first year at O.C., a black female counselor looked at my failure rate and decided that I was prejudiced against Hispanics, blacks, and Asians—exactly the people with the most writing difficulties (as unfair as that fact is). She called my chairman and wanted him to look into the matter. He good-naturedly told me about the complaint. Then he and Donna Smith stopped me from calling the counseling office to say, "I hear you people think I'm a racist. I want to talk to somebody—and not no woman nor minority. I want to talk to a white, Christian man." Later, though, I did tell a counselor that the counselor in question had left out Jews, Muslims, and women.

During my second year at O.C., former English teachers, coaches, concerned citizens, grandmas, and TV personalities begged me to change the grade of a hot-shot female basketball player. With an *F* changed to an Incomplete and then the Incomplete changed to *D,* she could then continue to play and get a scholarship to a high-class university. The argument was that I had "to consider the individual and her needs." I thought, when I gave her the *F,* that I was considering the individual and her needs. Eventually I gave into the phone calls and changed the grade for institutions and their needs. Students thus learn the easy lesson that they have no inner worth but are worth only their function in their society, their school, or their job.

But like some of the ladies mentioned above, some students made me proud of them because they taught me something. Through contact with them, no matter how meager, I think that maybe we shared something. A few students and I could squint and cock our heads to make the world look fuzzy, and we like our disparate fuzzy views better than the clear-eyed views that we're supposed to have. And by looking askance, we keep the world at bay even if and while it is incorporating us.

Some students have caused me problems but intrigued me and endeared themselves to me. In Oklahoma, during a summer school course in technical writing, my only female student, a black woman, dutifully waddled into class every day during the last month and a half of her pregnancy. A couple of days after the course had started, she told me that she might have the baby any time during the summer session. Toward the end of one particular class she tried to push herself up and out of her small desk but gasped and sank back into her seat. "I think this is it," she said. All the macho engineering, prevet, accounting, and agriculture majors cried in unison, "we don't know nothin' 'bout birthin' no babies" and left me with the woman. I called a fellow graduate teaching assistant who had been a nurse, and then I too left the room. Fortunately, the woman had had false labor pains.

In another class at O.S.U., during the first couple of days before I had learned names or faces, I walked into a class and saw a late paper lying on a podium. I went into my composition Nazi act and demanded that the owner of the paper remove it from my sight. We have departmental policy at O.S.U., I told the students. Slowly, from the back of the room, a young man pushed himself up from his desk. He had a cast from his fingers to his shoulder, propped up with a rod tied to his waist, and another cast from his thigh to his toes. I couldn't crack a smile, offer an apology, or excuse him without losing their respect and the strength of my threat. I stood stoically by as he slowly limped to the podium and grabbed the paper with the good hand, then limped back to his chair. He had nearly killed himself the night before in a car wreck. The whole class of tender young freshmen watched silently.

At O.C. I had a very bright man in my summer night class who was just slightly younger than I. He had written and apparently sold a TV script. But he had a habit of passing out midway through class. He was dead drunk, doped, or both. His classmates got used to his passing out. I didn't mind since he seemed to get the material anyway and didn't disturb anyone. One night he passed out and pissed his pants. I quickly gave the class its one and only break that entire semester. I tried to rouse the guy while attempting to keep my feet out of the puddle around his desk. I couldn't wake him. I thought that maybe he had had a stroke. I started to see myself in court, accused of boring someone to death. The other students came back into class and sat down. No one noticed anything until a local yokel from Kermit asked out loud, "What's that smell?" I tried to continue, but a woman sitting next to the incontinent guy raised her feet and wrinkled her nose, and the rest of the students in the class began to suppress giggles. I could not keep anybody interested in a lecture about cause and effect in writing. I called security. A patrolman, a custodian, and I finally roused this student, who thanked us and went home. He attended all of the remaining classes and didn't pass out the rest of the semester.

I'm not sure that the pregnant woman, the accident victim, or the guy with sleeping sickness learned anything, but they were concerned with matters far more important than grades (or even my class). They had some pressing problems, yet they never complained about my class or their needs. Each simply confronted the situation at hand. Furthermore, they all stuck the class out and kept their senses of humor. They had already learned a lot before they came into my class. Other students, I think, actually do benefit from what or how I teach.

Juan Maynez flipped over backward in his desk because of an epileptic seizure. A classmate crammed a pencil sideways into Juan's mouth to keep him from swallowing his tongue. I called a nursing instructor and dismissed the class. While the nursing instructor sat with Juan until he came to, I called the registrar to see if I could get any information. Juan had given the school a home address but no telephone number and no number to call in case of an emergency. Fortunately, he recovered and diligently continued to attend classes.

Though he rarely spoke, he wrote well, with a terse, no-nonsense sort of style. His first couple of essays began to intrigue me. From them, I learned that, when Juan was three, his parents literally pulled him across the Rio Grande as they "migrated" to America. He and his migrant parents then lived in a deserted boxcar in Pecos, Texas. Gradually they improved their living conditions and got Juan into the public schools, where he learned to speak English. Then he got himself a scholarship and a loan to go to Odessa College. Later I saw that Juan did very well with grammar. When I talked to him about his ability with grammar and his language, he told me that he had essentially taught himself English by memorizing the words, the orders, and the structures. As an elementary school student he would read, try to analyze the sentences grammatically, and then write some like them. When one of my Anglo students indignantly asked what use grammar had to anybody in the real world, I asked Juan to answer him. In the first words that he ever spoke in class, Juan said, "It's how I eat." Juan then told the class how he had learned to speak English. After that point in this class and in another class that Juan took with me, I always called on him in order to get him to talk and to hear what he had to say. I suspected that Juan knew and felt something that I never would. I could only glimpse his world now and then, maybe by looking askance. His world was far more profound than the academic and social world of my students, of the Odessa College counselors, and of Odessa College. And Juan's world gave him the strength to tolerate the O.C. world.

I had two students in class who wrote very poorly (though not through any fault of their own, I suspect), but they came to my sophomore literature class with a personally developed sense of tragedy and art. Tony Ontiveroz went to a series of literary readings that I had organized and afterward told me that he now realized he liked literature but still didn't like to read. Eluterio Garcia struggled to write a coherent essay in this sophomore literature class, but he did like the reading. He even thanked me for the course because it made him "feel more." I admired both students and felt sorry for them and angered at the system. I'm not sure who is to blame or if anyone is to blame. Both men were capable of far better writing and comprehension and thus better grades and greater chances of advancement to other colleges. But somewhere along the line, no one was tough enough or insistent enough to give them practice and thus firm understanding of structure and organization. But despite their inability with writing the language, both men felt deeply.

Ana Camacho did have ability, understanding, and the temperament. Married with two kids, Ana juggled her family through three of my classes, then through her junior and senior classes in English at U.T.P.B. She graduated as the outstanding English major at U.T.P.B. and got a job teaching in Ector County. For Ana, as for all of these students, literature meant something in her life. It was not some nice, moral commodity to be kept on a shelf or in a classroom. Ana once came into my office and told me that what she had learned in literature classes made her talk back to her priest. She had never really liked his dogmatic dictums about what is right or wrong according to church policy. So Ana, the good Chicana Catholic girl, told the priest that he was just a "man." And that meant that he was not God and could not understand as God understood and that he was not a woman and could not then understand as a woman understood. She was angered yet pleased. She told me that by reading literature she had become more of a feminist and a better Catholic.

As I stated in an earlier essay about Hispanicism in Texas, Ana was also my source for information about *curanderos,* Hispanic folk healers or witch doctors. I wanted to know about the local practitioners, and Ana, who rather guiltily admitted to her familiarity with curanderos, did some snooping and found out the addresses of and local legends about them. She said she knew that these magicians exploited poor people's ignorance and that they mixed up superstition and religion (not all that different to me). But still, she said, there was something there. She had been raised hearing about curanderos and had seen their cures and potions in her house. Her father had tragically been killed in an accident at a construction site, and among the local Hispanics rumors went around that some evil curandero had put a curse on the site. Ana was an intelligent and sophisticated woman before she came to college—sophisticated enough to sense a battle in her between what she knew and what she felt. She couldn't dismiss the beauty of the curandero legends and, though she did not blindly believe in Catholicism and curanderos, she didn't want to cut those parts of her past out of her heart or consciousness. She didn't want her daughter to know about all these superstitions and thus have them nag her, yet Ana felt guilty for cutting off a link between her daughter and her culture. It was a hard choice. Ana, to her credit, will have a lot of hard choices and see irony and complexity in these hard choices.

The Hispanic students, at least at the present, can have their Mexican world, exist in the Anglo world, and create their own personal worlds. No wonder they are assimilating. They possess some mystery and wonder that most Anglos will never know.

One African-American athlete, a basketball player, took several of my classes and impressed me with his mind and his attitude. Delbert Jones's main academic problem was that he was locked up with all the other athletes. He would goof off intentionally because his buddies did. But he always rescued his grade by writing an eloquent essay. The son of middle-class teachers, Delbert had such a sophisticated style that I first thought he had plagiarized papers. I still remember his insightful essay about how the term *jock* caused him to be labeled and misjudged more than the term *nigger.* The worst sort of prejudice, the most detrimental assumptions about jocks that Delbert had yet encountered were at O.C. A first-semester, eighteen-year-old freshman, Delbert saw that he was being manipulated. His coaches and the athletic system really had no concern for his personality or his interests. They didn't care what kind of grades he made, as long as he stayed eligible. Instructors, coaches, and counselors, when they learned that he was a "jock," discouraged him from taking any but the most basic classes and repeated words as though he could not understand literate English. He finally realized that all the school had given him was a place to stay, some free meals, and tuition money. His parents were able and willing to do as much for him and were far more concerned about his personal interests. The last year of his eligibility he sat the bench, cut practice, and otherwise became a detriment to the team, but he took the classes that he wanted to. Then he moved back to Dallas to go to a better school.

The toughest *D* I ever gave was Delbert's. When he came to my office to find out what he had made, I explained that he just hadn't quite pulled it out this time. The eloquence of his last essay hadn't excused the essay he had missed. He nodded his head, smiled, shook my hand, and told me that he was going back home to Dallas. After he walked out, I peeked out my office door and saw this big, muscular man swing one arm and snap his fingers, then lightly kick the wall.

The student whom I most liked at Odessa College was Tom Bailey because Tom Bailey looked at the world a lot like my drinking buddies. He knew a lot about psychopaths. A native of upstate New York, Tom quit college in the early seventies because it was a part of the establishment that he despised, grew his hair, and got various factory jobs. Tom quickly advanced in his workman jobs and became a leader in the union. But Tom, like my father, didn't like his Republican bosses with no wrinkles in their bellies. Rather than tolerating them at work and then cussing them at home, as my father did, and rather than trying to anger them or confound them as I did, Tom punched them out. Further, Tom liked to go to bars, and because he lived in a conservative part of the state, because he was big and intimidating, because he had hair over his shoulders and a long beard, he got into a lot of barroom fights. So Tom lost a lot of jobs and spent a lot of nights in jail. He learned that jail, the iron bar motel, was sort of a hotel for the poor. The rich could play within the legal system, but the workingman or poor man just spent his time in jail and then lost his job because he had cut work.

Tom eventually became a top hand in the West Texas oil patch. At thirty-three, Tom noticed that all his fingers were intact, that he had all his teeth, and that the metal had not bit him. The odds of reaching forty in the oil field with his teeth, fingers, and other body parts intact were against him. With his wife's support (Katie was a first grade teacher), Tom decided to try school again.

Tom was scrubbed, well-trimmed, and articulate in class. But when going over a paper out of class, he dismissed with all formal bullshit and said directly, "Now goddamn it, Jim, why can't I do this?" While he was in my American lit. class, we'd sometimes go out for a beer and exchange stories. I particularly enjoyed listening to a late-night barroom conversation between Tom and one of my creative writing students, an engineer and gunsmith of about fifty who wrote (and sold) stories about the differing methods and attributes of boxers and barroom brawlers.

Tom saw in literature, history, and government classes a central tension between headstrong individuals like himself and the powers that be. It was a fight that he had been involved in all his life. With some more education, he saw more comrades in his fight and learned new tactics. You got to fool the bastards. Tom graduated from U.T.P.B. as the top student (highest G.P.A., most honors) with a degree in government and got accepted into Oklahoma City University law school. But he only lasted in law school for three days.

Tom knew that law school was going to "kick his ass," but he didn't reckon that the social scene would kick his ass. He had left Katie and the two kids in Odessa, taken a bus to Oklahoma City, and reported to his dorm. At several dorm meetings, an old dorm mom and a troop of nineteen-year-old R.A.s told thirty-five-year-old, ex-barroom brawler Tom that he couldn't drink on campus or have booze in his dorm room, that he could not have females in his room (wife or otherwise), and that the R.A.s could inspect his room anytime they wished. And Tom, without a car, found out that the closest bar was ten blocks away. He went to the law dean and told him that he had already threatened to whip an R.A. and a couple of patrons in the one bar that he had found. The dean of the law school agreed to return Tom's tuition and dorm money if Tom left quickly. So Tom came back to Odessa. But this story ends happily: Tom got a job as an executive at a company designing products for the oil field. He got the job because the boss saw Tom's ability to talk with the hands and the management, his written and mental agility, and his hard-nosed attitude. At last report, I heard that Tom was wearing a suit and tie and black wing tips, carrying a briefcase, and giggling at himself.

Tom had the ability and intelligence to be a lawyer or professor, but he will help this society and culture more as an businessman. We really don't need any more psychopaths in academia or law. We don't need more people like me or Truett Hilliard ducking work by thinking. We need people like Tom, who can sympathize with us yet duke it out with the "real" world.

Tom and the students like him give me hope for education. But they and I know that I don't need them or a whole lot of hope to keep teaching. I'd rather teach than work, but I don't need teaching. And I think that I teach well because I don't need it and thus can find absurdity and humor in the sparks ignited among me, my students, and the subject matter. It is rewarding not because of what blue-haired old grammar teachers or commencement speakers say—sappy stuff like paving the way for our future, molding our society, helping young people—but because the unexpected, chaotic quality in it makes it amusing, funny, and thus the source for good anecdotes and stories. It provides a way to look askance at the world.

Women and Texas

Divorce in Odessa is quite common. While the men seemed plagued by many of the same problems and foibles as the women, the women seemed more interesting. Maybe I just liked listening to women's stories more; maybe I was just more prone to tolerating women's confessions. After reading C. W. Smith's moving essay about being a divorced father, "Uncle Dad," in *Esquire* (March, 1985, appearing later in hardcover, Putnam, 1987, and paper, Berkeley, 1989), I thought that I'd write a satire about dating divorced or nearly divorced women. "Dating" to me, in Odessa, concerned such changed tactics as hiding from the kids (or the husband, or the ex-husband, or friends of the husband), paying the baby-sitter, sneaking out of Mom's bedroom, going dutch when she can't afford it, getting used to the kids, etc. I became an observer but not a victim of the traumas of a sour marriage and divorce. Further, teaching at an urban community college, I had these women who were coping with divorce as students. So I gathered my nonstatistical data from these women.

These West Texas women represent, to me, the intersection of West Texas culture and education. These older than usual, nontraditional mothers attending school part-time put curves in the statistical charts about college students. And they form a large demographic chunk of consumers with certain schedules, economic and psychological needs, and new lifestyles. What most of these women have in common is the agonizing desire to make sense out of their lives after what they valued most—a husband and kids—are either gone or have dropped in status. If not biologically then psychologically, they have to push the fledglings, and the bastard who gave them fledglings, out of the nest.

These women haven't been planned for in Texas. They have few of the role models or examples that men have. The myth surrounding Texas is primarily a masculine myth. Like the black men that Mailer describes, women have not, until recently, had a stake in white, male culture; but on the other hand, unlike the black men, they have not been invisible. They have been incorporated into the myth. A woman had a cultural niche made for her, even in black culture and certainly in Hispanic culture.

While the roughneck might look back at a wild, frontier myth to nourish a sense of "self," a woman could not and cannot retain her society's sense of femininity and also become a frontiers"man." Further, modern-day frontiersmen have the precedent and the nearly admired option of deserting family to head off into the wilds for further self-expression. Willy Loman yearns to go out west in order to become a more fulfilled Emersonian man—just like his father, who deserted the family; just like Ben, who runs from the family; and just like tormented Biff, who has no family. In *Lonesome Dove* Clara scolds Woodrow Call for ruining her chance of a fulfilling life with Gus. With Call always starting some foray into the wilderness, Gus would never have stuck at home on a horse farm like Clara's. The oil field worker or the military man can periodically leave home to go out with the boys to the rig, maybe off-coast or all the way to a third world country, or go off on maneuvers, or shove off with the fleet. A man could achieve social stature and reward for maintaining civilization *or* for running off to the wilderness. The woman can only tend the home fires. Even Whitman, when he praises women in "Song of Myself," adds a qualifier that regulates women to men's place for them: "And I say it is as great to be a woman as to be a man, / And I say there is nothing greater than the mother of men."

A woman, in our myths, has no alternatives. She is always defined. Women always were responsible for maintaining the feminine virtues of family, tradition, and church. These are "feminine" virtues because they complement or supplement masculine virtues, and thus as "complements" or "supplements" they help to define male roles. In Odessa, Texas, the woman's role is even more strictly defined and policed. Marriage is crucial. A woman needs to supplement a man in order to have any worth. By the time they are out of high school or in their early twenties, women are either married or have been married. Kids too are important. I knew twenty-year-olds in Odessa who got pregnant because they "needed" to have kids.

No wonder then that twentieth-century American women, especially in West Texas, are neurotics and have a slim chance of locating any psychopathic impulses to stimulate their growth. Maintaining house, home, family, and Christianity; delivering the kids to school in the Suburban; attending Junior League Meetings; and making out the Christmas cards leave little time for drinking, carousing, or some feminine psychopathy. In fact, I can't even think of myths, precedents, or anecdotes (except those about prostitutes) that support a woman's psychopathic abandonment. Many of the "liberated" women whom I see offer no real solution. So many just exchange one load of neuroses for another. They become feminine men and support the "ism" at hand and end up with a big chip on their shoulders trying to be as good as any man. Others live a life of example rather than a real life; they plan every move to exhibit an enlightened or liberated womanhood, and thus say and do things that sound as mannered and artificial as any Junior League, Baptist accountant's wife.

So a woman has a much harder time breaking the habits of family and church because she has no alternative examples. And by the time she is mature, her whole life has been conditioned. If she breaks out, she is a true emotional pioneer. Her struggle is harder than a man's and therefore dearer. When a woman does succeed at self-definition, she is more beautiful than the man who has done the same. To come to understanding, a woman pushes into uncharted territory and feels the wonder (like the wonder of the Dutch sailors in *The Great Gatsby* who first glimpsed the New World) of making her own narrative, which might become myth to her granddaughters. Like the Hispanic, the twentieth-century Texas and American woman may be creating twenty-first-century myths. Going to the local college campus, especially *after* wifery and motherdom, is one way she might push into uncharted territory. These older than normal, returning women students are the real women's movement.

Unfortunately, for many women college learning is just like church. It is an extension of male supplementing, just more definitions. Many women who return to college do so to help with their husbands' careers, and thus they remain merely a supplement to their husbands and those husbands' really important work. Or they come to college to give themselves something to do. It gets boring sitting alone at home in the middle of a cultural wasteland. Or they come to college for psychological therapy, something cheaper (and less honest) than an analyst, which will give them a self-enhancing boost. Community college counseling centers are composed of counselors who subscribe to this latter theory of education.

Others have left husbands and thus, in their eyes, have failed because they couldn't hold their men. They no longer offer anything of value to their male-dominated culture. They desperately need some sort of definition. School offers them another neurosis, another way of robbing them of autonomy and forcing them into a different mold. These women become the grade-chasers. Grades take the place of husbands or conventions or husbands' orders; grades now define these women and justify their existence. Their psyches become so delicate that they shatter when they receive *C's*. *C's* place these women in the dung heap composed of the normal and the mediocre; no longer do they have some special, innate quality just by the fact that they are individuals. They hope for a sense of self without ever inspecting self either through sensuality or study. They have a much better chance of breaking through to some sense of self by going to the bars.

College, though, for some, offers vicarious experience: the chance through imagination or identification to relive a part of their lives. They become aware of the distinction between "truth" and social convention. "Truth" becomes something dearer, perhaps something nonexistent, but whatever their philosophical development, those who are able to learn and not just make grades see an enlarged self and a smaller world. I think it a positive step, then, that these women reexamine their home lives, their husbands, perhaps even their children, at whatever cost to family life, society, or old myths; they are ripe now for visits to the bar and for a few affairs.

Any seduction and any affair carries the potential for destruction, but it also carries the possibility for liberation. Extramarital booze and sex, if done with the addition of beauty, offer a woman another chance at a more profound and personal beauty than the sentimental, cloying things that she was told were beautiful when she married.

But because she feels so isolated, those shallow and easily learned sentimental truths always nag at her. With beauty must come the chance for tragedy and destruction, so the educated woman, whether she has gone to college or not, risks a lot. She is tempted to regress and search not for beauty but for the security of old ideas. But she has now lost faith in those old ideas; she can never see them as she used to; she can never again really live according to their dictates. She is in a precarious position. Another lover or husband is usually the easy answer.

Joan and Charla showed up in my classes about the same time. Both had good lives and, in my opinion, friendly husbands who also became my friends. Each husband was husband number two. Both women had married early in standard West Texan fashion. Joan's husband had a wife behind him, and Charla's had several. Everybody had kids. Joan and Chris, though, through some sort of quirk or luck had only one. Both ladies were bright and took to writing, then literature. Both took whatever courses struck their fancy, whatever complemented not their husbands but their newly discovered selves. Joan is the student who told me that she only liked the "selfish" courses.

At the time, I was teaching a lot of night classes, so Joan and Charla got together with other friends, other "older" coeds, and all of them ended up in my classes. In one particular American literature class, my largely over-thirty female class and I were learning about Americans (it was a class in which Emerson and Mailer and Turner started to make sense to me through examples right in front of me). Joan and Charla and their contingency were enthusiastic about the class, asked questions before class, and joined me for drinks afterward. They sat in a group on one side of the classroom. On the other side of the class were students whom Joan and Charla didn't recruit: several Pentecostal women (I could tell by their hair), a man who brought his Bible to class, and some other, I assume, churchy types. All of them liked to bring God into the class discussions. In Odessa, Texas, I mostly liked to leave God alone.

While studying Walt Whitman, a real litmus test author for potential sensualists, Charla got especially intrigued. She came to see me before class and asked me about certain passages of "Song of Myself" because she couldn't believe what she was reading. She was overjoyed that such racy stuff was in college instead of the staid, moral lessons she got in high school literature class. During the discussion of Whitman, Charla squirmed in her seat and extolled Whitman's sensuality and how it made her feel. I did my best to tone down my own and Charla's comments. But Charla was caught up on the sexuality. "Jim, tell us about where he is 'doing it' with the horse," Charla said. Her friends turned around to look at her. The Good Christians turned up their noses, and I stuttered. Charla went on to say, "Here is the homosexual stuff. Here he's doing it with trees. . . ." Because of her enthusiasm, she did a much better job of presenting the poem than I had ever done.

One of the Pentecostal women, who had no doubt learned something in the previous composition and literature course, said that Whitman was just being metaphoric: "Whitman was just using the . . ."—here the woman hesitated to find the right word—"sex to illustrate his main points about feeling." Charla was undaunted and not about to be checked. "No, No, Whitman doesn't mean to be metaphoric," Charla said. "That's the point. He wants us experiencing everything in the same way that we fuck." The following week, everyone but the one male, Charla, Joan, and their friends dropped the class.

Within the year, Charla filed for divorce from Bruce, and in like fashion, Joan filed for divorce from Chris. Both women had settled into a major or at least an interest. Surprisingly to me, Charla became interested in biology and chemistry, completed her study at U.T.P.B., and got accepted into medical school. Joan became interested in photography and dedicated most of her time and study to the dark room in O.C.'s photography department. Both, I thought, had become more beautiful and intriguing than they had ever been.

In another year, both had new men. Joan discovered sex with the wrong person. She drifted into and out of an affair with a married man who always promised to leave his wife for her. By the time he had moved in with Joan, she had spent most of her divorce settlement and had failed all of her classes. She simply stopped going to class and didn't bother to simply drop them. Charla, of all improbabilities, married a very strict Baptist. Extramarital sex was okay only if you felt guilty afterward. I had a discussion about "God," religion, and science with Charla. Basically, I couldn't believe that she, like some instructors at O.C., could apparently square a personal, feel-good, noncontingent God with a naturalistic, quantum-physical, subatomic, contingent scientific universe. Charla agreed with me and said that she missed some of our conversations, but she said that simple Baptist theology "makes you feel good because it just makes everything so comfortable, definite, and simple."

"And, boring," I added. I knew and she knew that she really couldn't believe it. But she was committed to her new man and thus to his guilt and neurosis.

As for Joan, I believe that the last beau I met was a "stay against chaos." She needed to break out of neat metrical forms and defend her own free verse for a little longer. But just the *fact* of a man was comforting to Joan. She was once again proving that she could indeed feel as she could in the first years of her marriage. She had broken out of the habitual, and so anyone who gave his attention to her would look strange, exotic, and fantastic. For both Joan and Charla, the comforts of the past won out over the glories but dangers of the orgiastic present. Their neurosis won out over their psychopathy. Safety won out over possible destruction. The older I get, the more I sympathize with them. More recently I talked to both. Joan seems to be prospering in Odessa, and Charla was in residency.

Holding on to a hard-won self, for a woman, is almost more difficult than the winning. Without the precedents, without the applause or accolades, without male vocational ambitions, self-discovery seems so much harder than surrendering. Sometime, in the future, Joan and Charla will again repeat their past, because their comforts will grow old or boring, and they will again yearn for an emotional, aesthetic, and intellectual orgiastic present. Maybe this predicament is inevitable for all of us.

Some women do hold on to self. Three women in my fiction-writing classes came from different backgrounds and had interests other than in literature but found, in writing fiction, a means to heighten self. Ironically for them, in a way that counselors, neurotics, and many creative writing students don't understand, playing with the language was therapeutic. One was happily married and held down her job as a geologist. She, of course, though, was older and a native of New York. Another was happily unmarried. And another was, like I was, happily neurotic because she was young and wanted to be a writer. And there was Ana Camacho, who made all the literary readings that I sponsored, even brought her daughter, and has let the study of literature strengthen her life and her family. Her daughter liked literary readings and literature. Thus her daughter developed an interest in something and has an example in her mother. The last I heard, Ana's daughter was vying for a scholarship from some college far from Odessa.

I think that men who value sensuality and beauty have glimpsed such women or dream about them. And this is one reason why men "run" with women. They search for one who has beaten her environment to find herself. Even if a woman has not won or not yet won, her struggle to establish her own identity is so nearly tragic that it makes her beautiful. Men flirt with all women who show this kind of potential, and men hope to find one who can stretch the sensual beauty into sexual beauty.

All of this beauty is why I like the company of women. Truett Hilliard and I often talk about ladyfriends, wives, and women in general. Truett is an expert in the Romanticism surrounding women. I am an apprentice.

Perhaps my interest is hereditary. After my grandmother died, my seventy-year-old maternal grandfather had a series of "ladyfriends." While my grandfather was living down the block from my family, he would eat supper with us. At eighty, still a vain man, always looking at his well-combed hair, always sprinkling baby powder on himself, my grandfather showed up at our table one night with a hangdog face and announced that one of his ladyfriends down at his club had said he was "losing his looks." Several weeks later, he announced that he was "a dead man."

A month or two later, at eighty-one, he was dead. He had nothing to live for; he could no longer hunt (his other passion), and the blue-haired old ladies no longer liked him. Before he died, my father claimed that my grandfather's blue-haired ladyfriends were killing him. My father meant to insult my grandfather. He meant to say that my grandfather shouldn't let what silly old women say weigh in the balance. But I think that my grandfather had a good death, a timely death, if in fact he died because the ladies lost interest in him and he conversely lost interest in them. He had had a full life, and neither he nor I would have liked to have seen it ruined by prolonged sickness, senility, or intolerable crotchetiness.

I am luckier than my grandfather because I have a job in which I interact with women. It is a bird nest on the ground. Truett often says that everything is done for seductive purposes. We can be seduced and we can seduce because we can see beauty. We crave it as well as power, and we can see beauty and power everywhere, especially in college teaching. Teaching is sexy because it is sensual—especially in the "selfish" courses. Even the boys down at Marie's knew this and envied Truett, Barry, and me. And I teach a subject that depends upon emotion and sensuality. In teaching literature, I am exploring the sensual as well as the logical or philosophical. To people unaccustomed to thought, a mixture of philosophy and sensuality is intoxicating.

In dealing with language, I am dealing with something that is very close to a person's assumptions about himself. Some students have yet to make the distinction between themselves and their language. The best advice that I can give to the single men who hang out in the fancy, disco-country bars (lounge lizards or, as West Texas girls say, "horny toads") is to study language. The sophisticated use of language will convince those smart women who have yet to figure out the difference between linguistics and reality that you are wise and sensual. The bourgeoisie, in this age of functional illiteracy and literary ignorance, will see an ability to manipulate language of some technical skill much like the ability to perform surgery or fit pipes. Both types will be impressed. Those simple people who see language as neither wisdom nor technical expertise are beyond us. And those more enlightened women who see a distinction between reality and language are immune to the verbal charms of glib lounge lizards and other men. They are probably doing some of their own seducing.

Women in West Texas are especially susceptible to the well-turned phrase. West Texas men assume that linguistic dexterity is best kept at home with the ol' lady, the church, and school. You bullshit with your buddies, not with the ol' lady. Conversations with her are less fun and more serious. And because a man who can manipulate the language is rare, West Texas women like men who can keep pace with a woman's ability to bullshit.

Thus the teaching of English and other liberal or fine arts, maybe even science, becomes sensual, and thus intense emotions are aroused. They should be, because otherwise no one grows, no one learns. Sexuality lurks all about. Every liberal arts instructor, whether male or female, could be accused of sexual harassment. Most of us would be up on charges if it were not for the facts that most of our students don't learn and most of our students are so sexless.

A ladyfriend of Truett's commented that he and his drinking buddies seemed "so free." Coming from a Church of Christ background, bound for fifteen years to a rigid husband, and just getting back to school, she knew nothing but limitations, so to her, our crowd seemed free. My buddies accepted our ineffectiveness and reveled in it, so to some extent we *were* free.

Freedom, abandonment, wildness acts as an emotional aphrodisiac to the right kind of women. At the mercy of male prejudices about what women should be; at the mercy of institutional prejudices, bad marriages, and the myths they had been told as girls, these women see freedom as something dangerous yet exciting. Through taking our classes; through going into a bar, a real or metaphoric one, unescorted; through reading hence forbidden or uninteresting stuff; through having the obligatory affair or even imagining it, they get vicarious or real experience. The freedom attracts them yet scares them and eventually makes them more complete as self-defined women. Maybe they can etch out their own myth so that future women may have a more vicarious means to deal with intellectual seduction and liberation.

Conclusions?

I hope that I have looked at Emerson's romantic notions about self and Mailer's notion about psychopaths and neurotics, which reflects Emerson, and the place where self works itself out in America, for better and worse—out on the frontier, or more specifically in Texas, or even more specifically in Odessa. Tired of academic papers and sometimes losing the distinctions between fiction and nonfiction, I turned to the world around me, which happened to be culture and education in West Texas, to illustrate my points. Needless to say, then, these essays have become more and more autobiographical. Maybe I'm telling more about me than about West Texas. So I almost feel as though I should apologize to anyone who has read this far.

I have made certain assumptions about me and my writing through writing these essays. Though I claim to be a romantic in the introduction, I'm stuck in a realist's position with these essays. Out of a multitude of sensations, I grope through certain ones and label those as experience. From this experience, I then manipulate the facts by organizing them or sifting through them to make true or untrue stories. This is similar to what Henry James means when he talks about "selection." Like any writer, then, I am constantly making meaning out of experience. And perhaps, like the realists, I am slightly plagued by the fact that I carry this narrative technique around with me and thus constantly impose meaning on experience. I am, though, unlike W. D. Howells and some other of my heroes, able to soothe myself. And unlike journalists and some of my students, I am not at all concerned about objectivity.

I am postmodern enough to distrust my meaning or anyone's meaning, though I am Spinozaistic enough to want desperately to find meaning wherever I look. No writer and perhaps no human with any degree of intellect can live a completely existential life because we are constantly imposing meaning on ourselves or our world, or we are constantly looking for meaning in what has just happened (so much for Mailer, the basis of many of these essays). As Gabriel Marcel says, we are busy "recollecting" or "*re*-collecting." The writer just can't help this juggling. But I'm not quite egotistical enough to think that I've come up with some exact truth. I distrust truth too much. I hope, though, that I have created some vicarious sensation in readers. Truett Hilliard says that he would rather live a beautiful life than a moral one. He is succeeding. To do so, you have to look at the world "askance." I hope that I have looked askance and created some beautiful essays rather than some true ones. As far as a tight and consistent logic in the essays, I'll defend myself by quoting Whitman: "Do I contradict myself? / Very well then I contradict myself," though I contain only multitudes of Texas, or multitudes of what some Texans would call bullshit (as opposed to horseshit).

I keep thinking of catchy phrases to paraphrase my points here: "To believe your own thought, to believe that what is true for you in your private heart, is true for all men—that is true genius"; "Whoso would be a man must be a nonconformist"; "Your goodness must have some edge to it—else it is none. The doctrine of hatred must be preached as the counteraction of the doctrine of love when that pulses and whines. I shun father and mother and wife and brother, when my genius calls me. I would write on the lintels of the doorpost, *Whim.*" I'm not sure if I got these slogans from Emerson or from Reebok athletic shoe commercials. Emerson wrote some convoluted essays but some great one-liners. He would have been a great adman. But besides making copy for what used to be plain ol' tennis shoes, Emerson's pithy one-liners got absorbed into American character and character*s*. And Texans are a subspecies of Americans and yet super-Americans (and West Texans and thus Odessans are super-Texans). They reveal Emerson's advice come to fruition. It seems that, just as in Emerson's day, Americans, as exemplified by West Texans, battle between self and those things that impede self, between those people sitting in front of pulpits or those sitting in front of bars. Both sides are contained in the label *Texan* and in the myth that surrounds Texas.

I think that what I have said is surely what a lot of Texans and most every teacher know. From eighteenth-century agrarian thought, Jefferson and Franklin dreamed of a rural society where land meant prosperity and thus gave the owner time for leisure and sober reflection. He could then turn to civic matters and help his country by serving as a representative and by voting correctly. Emerson makes nature the conduit to God, and Whitman mixes emotional and physical with nature, "love-root, crotch and vine." So in the nineteenth century, land became holy and personal. After the census of 1890 reported that we were out of land, Frederick Jackson Turner, Henry Nash Smith, and good ol' Walter P. Webb saw deep ramifications on our psyches. Most Texans, though, don't read Turner, Webb, or Smith. The land and the myth that it created haven't worn out in the minds of Texans.

First settled when Emerson was becoming a transparent eyeball, developed at the height of manifest destiny, Anglo Texas gelled as a mixture of American romanticism and its cousin American land lust. Even if we are running out of land, we deny it. Everybody in Texas wants a piece of land. And we let another great American passion couple with our lust for land—money. With the later nineteenth-century Horatio Alger myth, crass, shallow wealth could take the place of holy land, of nature, of communing with God, of civic pride and responsibility. So one of the most influential people in Texas, as deemed by no less an authority than *Texas Monthly,* is H. Ross Perot, not so much because of what he has done but because of his money. But as soon as a Texan has money, he wants land, not public land but rather *his* land.

Maybe because Texas *was* so big (yes, it has gotten smaller in the twentieth century), maybe because it was its own country, Texans retain a more vivid sense of identity with their locale (I don't know if I could live where I couldn't find a good enchilada). Texans give into the pursuit of property and money more than other Americans. At the basis is land; and not just land, but what happened on the land is important to Texans. All the heroism, grand deeds, cheating, deceit, murder, and theft that took place among Americans, Mexicans, Indians, and Spaniards on Texas land make land a commodity that might somehow give a present Texan a piece of myth or a sense of the tragic and poetic. And even if a Texan doesn't *own* land, he still *has* it by living in Texas. Even transplanted Texans can *have* this sense of land because the myth has taken over. You don't have to own Enchanted Rock to get a mixture of thrill, adventure, pride, and indignation when you read the plaque at the top about how Jack Hays stood off a dozen or so Comanches (even if present-day historians refute that myth, I want to believe it. On my latest trip to Enchanted Rock, I couldn't find this plaque. The park worker couldn't tell me where it was. The new Enchanted Rock State Park, promoted as a geological archive, has no place for it or all the politically incorrect and volatile history behind it. It is a record not just for Jack Hays and the unnamed Comanches but for all the trouble and violence in our past and for our changing views of our past. It is a monument *to* us too. I want it back.)

So even a city boy like Michael Zinberg or me feels the land and wants to preserve it by preserving the myths, even if he preserves or creates city myths arising out of Dallas, Houston, San Antonio, or El Paso. But because the myth sometimes surrounds him, because he also knows that there were tactical blunders and Anglo chauvinism at the Alamo, because the myth is so outlandishly macho, because the goddamn thing at times just won't let him go, the Texan, whether male or female, hates it and tries to escape. But as soon as he puts distance between the myth and himself through education, sophistication, or geography, he misses it. I purposefully leave out feminine pronouns here because I think that the pull is such a gonad-clanging, macho thing. So for good and bad, for men and women, the Texas myth, arising out of the land, even though the land and the myth may be used up, gives us a sense of tragedy. The myth may lead an individual to Emersonian self-enlightenment, or Maileresque psychopathic growth, or a neurotic fundamentalist repression. And thus we can see or feel beauty in one of the ugliest areas of the country.

Truett Hilliard can go a step further. He likes to try to feel the rocks. He likes to try to feel the desert Southwest and its complete obliviousness to humans and their myths. He too, then, a Portales, New Mexican, is bound to the land.

In 1989, because I didn't like teaching in a community college, I interviewed for a job at a four-year liberal arts college in Portland, Oregon. The Northwest had unusually cold, brilliant, crystalline weather. So this South Texas boy got to walk in snow, stare at real mountains through clear air, and drive to wineries, breweries, and orchards. The students had very high S.A.T.s, wore berets, and seemed genuinely interested in literature. Many were creamy-skinned, black-haired Polynesians radiating health. Ironically, during two of the nights that I spent there, in a cold motel room with windows fogging and then freezing over, I watched the first episodes of the network premiere of *Lonesome Dove.* I thought that, by God, Robert Duvall, Tommy Lee Jones, and Bill Wittliff got it right. They followed Larry's directions and fleshed out those characters. I knew those characters; I could see them out in West Texas; a part of me was still them.

On the flight home through that brilliant winter air, I pressed my face against the window of the plane and looked at the tops of the snow-covered Rockies. This was rich stuff. But I was most impressed when the plane flew across the Llano Estacado, which was an endless, even blanket of white. When I landed back in bleak, ugly Odessa, I thought that I had just been to fantasyland but that I was back to what I was, what I knew. I all but knew that I wouldn't get the job in Oregon; I didn't feel fated to be conversing with smart people in a pleasant, educated, and sophisticated area.

But I eventually left Odessa. As I mentioned, because the institution kept me from continued conflict and thus from more chances to "fuck off," as Donna Smith says, I started looking for other jobs the moment I got to Odessa College. So I eventually got one, not in the cold, frozen tundra north of the Red River, but just across the state, in East Texas, in Beaumont.

That yuppie guide for living *Places Rated* ranks Odessa as one of the worst places to live in the country. Beaumont is a bit higher rated. As my poet partner, Sam Gwynn said, when I was hired, I was one of the most valuable employees at Lamar because the university had to go through a nationwide search to find someone for whom Beaumont and Lamar were a step up. I feel a kind of pride at living in such detestable places. Maybe I should move to Pine Bluff, Arkansas.

Beaumont is more of the Old South in Texas. Writer Clay Reynolds says that if Louisianans could figure out how to work a winch, they'd attach it to Beaumont and pull it back to Louisiana where it belongs. Like the plains Indians who got spooked by the Rockies, like the longtime West Texas residents who feel claustrophobic when they see trees around them, I feel easier in more open country. In Southeast Texas, I feel like one of Santa Anna's cavalry troopers. I have let Sam Houston's Anglo woodsmen draw into their woods, and dismounted, with no clear ground to charge across, I am about to be picked off. Once a year I like to drive through clearer, sparser ranch country.

Driving out of the dark, humid East Texas piney woods, past Houston,

I always feel a vague sense of relief. When you drive seventy or eighty in East Texas, trees pass by too fast; I want to look off of the road and see some space. Mesas, hills, arroyos sit out at a distance and stay outside your windshield for a while. In West Texas we need the seventy-mile speed limit, but seventy is too fast to drive to keep up with the trees in East Texas. They zoom by, and you can't get a good view of them. The rolling green prairies west of Houston invite a seventy-mile speed limit (along with the Houston drivers). The prairies, with their stands of trees, *like* the farmers and ranchers who settled there. It is gentle country. You should look as you pass by it. Go seventy but not eighty. Save eighty for West Texas.

Yet Beaumont feels a little like Texas because it is not clearly any area. San Antonio, sitting astride Balcones Fault, besides being on the border between Hispanic and Anglo Texas, is also on the border between farming and ranching Texas. Most of Texas, with no distinct landscape of its own other than perhaps the trans-Pecos region, is a large transition zone. Texas lies between high plains and Mexican desert, southern forests and Texas coastal plains, coastal plains and Edwards Plateau. And it lies between Mexico, the American Southwest, the American South, and the Midwest. As a Texan, I may have transition in my nature.

I can feel that a place is home, but I can't feel at home in it. Larry McMurtry says that he likes to drive because of his herding instinct. He says that writing is like herding words. In Beaumont, I am restless; I drive a lot—to the same bars and hangouts, like the Border Patrol agents out tracking the signs, like the illegal immigrants they chase, like a roughneck going to the next rig, like his wife and kids following him, like a herder, like those solitary, celibate characters I first admired in the movies, like the ones I teach about in American literature. We roam in all kinds of ways, maybe looking for a home, scared of finding it because of what it may cost us, hoping that the company, the bullshit, or the taste of that first beer will be enough. What else is going to graduate school, a move to another town, and yearning for that next job, town, bar, woman, man, story, adventure? Variations on a theme. So we "beat on, boats against the current, borne ceaselessly into the past."

Truett Hilliard, despite the fact that he claims to be New Mexican, in good Texas fashion came up with an analogy for my leaving Odessa. It's the closest thing I will have yet come to a divorce, Truett says. I want to get away from the old lady, Odessa College and some other institutions, but I don't want to leave the kids.

Now I know that I'll always want to run away from the old lady, whichever one I'm presently married to, partially because Odessa showed me that I have a hard time living with my old ladies, but thank the Lord that playing with the kids makes her bearable. I miss the Odessa kids.